'If you're considering getting a dog; or have one already and need some advice, this is a great book, full of useful, interesting and practical tips!'
– *Julian Norton, aka The Yorkshire Vet, veterinary surgeon and author*

'If you want to know all about your pooch – fetch this. Inspiring, warm and practical guide to cohabiting with your canine.'
– *Russell Kane, comedian*

'This book is full of practical, heartfelt advice for both new and experienced dog owners. Dogs have long been human's best friend and this book helps us to benefit even more from this relationship. Your furry friend will thank you!'
– *The Reverend Canon Kate Bottley*

In memory of Angel, my beautiful Dobermann
– the reason I am where I am today

HAPPY DOG, HAPPY YOU

A positive guide to a joyful relationship with your dog

Verity Hardcastle

First published in Great Britain in 2023 by Yellow Kite
An imprint of Hodder & Stoughton
An Hachette UK company

1

A CIP catalogue record for this title is available
from the British Library

Hardback ISBN 978 1 399 70267 6
eBook ISBN 978 1 399 70268 3

Typeset in Sabon by Goldust Design

Printed and bound in Great Britain by Clays Ltd, Elcograf S.p.A.

Hodder & Stoughton policy is to use papers that
are natural, renewable and recyclable products and
made from wood grown in sustainable forests. The logging
and manufacturing processes are expected to conform to
the environmental regulations of the country of origin.

Yellow Kite
Hodder & Stoughton Ltd
Carmelite House
50 Victoria Embankment
London EC4Y 0DZ

www.yellowkitebooks.co.uk

CONTENTS

INTRODUCTION

I'm Verity Hardcastle. I am a certified Master Groomer, a member of the Guild of Master Groomers, a groomer by trade, a dog handler and all-round dog aficionado. Put simply, I am dog obsessed. I come from a long line of dog fanatics on both my maternal and paternal side, so I blame the genetics!

My late paternal grandad was a record-holding gundog trainer, who dedicated his life to his dogs, among other country pursuits. When he wasn't out training his dogs in his plus fours and paisley cravat, he'd be down the garden with them. They were all kennelled working dogs who only came inside when they were very elderly. I remember them well – the smell of their food and that clean kennel scent. In contrast, my maternal grandparents and great-grandparents were all dog fanciers who snuck their dogs titbits at the table and let them sleep on their beds. They also owned everything in twos – from Tibetans to Norfolks and Dalmatians to Lhasas.

Dogs have always been a mainstay of my family life and, historically, I don't think there has been a family member without a dog by their side.

A Bit About Me . . .

I've adored animals from as far back as I can remember. Some of my earliest memories involve car journeys where I'd play guess the dog breed as I obsessively went through my A–Z of breeds, thrilled if I spotted one out of the norm. I would spend all my pocket money on Puppy in my Pocket toys, I would daydream about Chihuahuas (lovely as they are, that was a passing phase, thanks to Paris Hilton) and, later, go bananas whenever I saw a Dobermann, my favourite breed of dog in my late teens. So much so that when I wasn't allowed a big dog, being the sassy young adult I was, there was only one thing for it: I saved up and left home at the age of eighteen – just so I could become the lucky custodian of a Dobermann. Mad, right? At the time, I thought I was so grown up – an adult, in fact – but now, at the ripe old age of thirty-seven, I can see that I was still a child. I no longer recognise that younger version of myself, but it was a journey I had to take, and one that led to me to where I am today.

That Dobermann was Angel. She died at the grand old age of thirteen and a half. She was and ever will be my heart dog. She was the reason I am sitting here, writing this, and the reason my career has been dedicated to something I wholeheartedly love. We went through so much together – the ups and downs of life. I was so lucky and blessed to have had her at my side through the bad times and the good: she was there when I found love, she was in my bridal party (I kid you not – she wore a white flower garland around her neck and disrupted the service, as she wanted to be next to me and my husband), she was there when I became a mother . . . Through the many metamorphoses of life, Angel was my rock, my everything. Hence this book is in her memory.

A Dobermann's not really a beginner's dog, but I was already fairly experienced and had also read lots of books, and Angel's breeder was a show breeder who took me under her wing. My plan was to show this Dobermann, which would set me on the path to where I am now. Of course, there were plenty of calamities along the way. I remember early recall issues nearly ending in disastrous consequences, moments when I totally embarrassed myself in the show ring by accidentally leaving a liver trail around the ring, sending other competitors' dogs berserk. Fun times! But we're all always learning, aren't we? We have to be able to laugh at ourselves and, believe me, at times I'm a hoot!

I found dog grooming to be the scratch to my itch – and one that also pays my bills (because sadly, we can't just cuddle dogs all day, heavenly as that would be). Following a taster-day grooming, I enrolled at a school and threw myself into it wholeheartedly. So much so that after gaining my initial qualifications, I decided that I wasn't going to be just any old groomer – I wanted to be the best goddam groomer I could be. So I set about training with as many people I admired as possible. If there was an area I wasn't so great at, I would focus on that. I wanted to be an all-rounder, understanding all breeds, all coat types, all behaviours. I took part in grooming competitions all over the UK and in America. I won many and I lost some – but whatever happened, I always took something away from the ex-perience. Dog guardianship in all aspects is a learning curve; every misdemeanour will provide a lesson, and how we grow is what's important.

With my love of Dobies, I used to think of myself as a big-dog kinda gal but, as I hit my twenties, I fell in love with Miniature and Toy Poodles, which was a pretty big U-turn. It's their hair, their wicked sense of fun, their wonderful intelligence, their loving and fun personalities; and, despite their fluffy hairdos, they are still proper dogs, with bags of energy, enthusiasm and charisma. I currently have four of the fluffheads, but I'm positive you'll find a poodle at my feet or tucked under my bingo wing even when I'm a very young-at-heart and rather beautiful eighty-year-old.

... and a Bit About Dogs

Going back over 40,000 years, wolves were wild and in direct competition with us for food and territory, but then there was a shift, when this now extinct species of wolf started to come into contact with and live around humans, becoming more used to us.

Around 20–40,000 years ago, dogs became domesticated, gradually transitioning from their wild ancestors to the ball-fetching, sheep-herding, snuggly cuddle buddies we know today. Some of the first domesticated wolves in Europe didn't survive and their lineage cannot be found in the modern-day dog, so it looks like different wild dog populations interbreeding with wild wolves meant that early dog species were replaced over thousands of years. Fossils from the Bronze Age suggest there were five groups of dogs in existence: wolf-type dogs, mastiffs, sighthounds (great for speed), herding dogs (for working with livestock) and pointing dogs (a hunter's helper). Domestication of dogs was happening all over the world and, from those early wolves, dogs have evolved through selective breeding,

whereby humans have picked the characteristics of certain dogs to breed on, whether for looks, or, originally, most likely for temperament, to create the wonderful array of breeds and mixes we see today. No other land species is as diverse as the dog; there is literally a dog out there for everyone, whether you like long legs or stumpy ones, big ears or tiny little lugs. It's insane to think of the dog as one species when they can be so different in looks and temperament. Take the Great Dane, for example – smooth, strong, weighing in at about 70kg; then compare that to the fuzzy, foxy Pomeranian at only about 3kg. Understanding 'dog' and how each and every one is so different in looks and behaviour is vital, as each is unique.

We have always liked, needed and wanted dogs around us, whether for pure friendship or as a status symbol (as in ancient Greek times when they were kept as companions as well as protectors and hunters, through to the Palace of Versailles). Dogs have been working for us for thousands of years and still do so today. I live in North Yorkshire and around me, in the Yorkshire Dales, I see Collies riding on the backs of quad bikes, as farmers' helping hands and tractor companions. I see Labradors readying themselves for a day in the field retrieving game. Then there are those that do herding and search and rescue, there are guide dogs (you can now have a cuddle party with a pack of Retrievers – divine!) and there are therapy dogs, who go into residential homes and shower people with their joyous love and good-vibes-only aura or into hospitals to visit people young and old, providing a dog snug and silent understanding. And let's not forget the police dogs we see working so hard at airport terminals. Dogs are givers and deserve our respect, having performed thankless tasks for us for centuries with wagging tails and enthusiasm, and all for little more than a simple need for a warm bed, food and praise. And there are a lot of lessons we can learn from them in our modern world – not least about doing a good deed without the need or want for thanks. So it's our duty to try to understand them more and be the best guardians we can possibly be. In return, we will have a calm, happy, balanced four-legged pal at our side.

A dog's legacy is something they can never know but, as the custodians of these incredible creatures, *we* know, and *we* understand. That's why they mean so much to us and have been around humans and their households for thousands of years. And that's why they deserve the best of us.

Happy You, Happy Dog: What's It All About?

Working with dogs and being around them 24/7 has really helped me to tune in to their behaviour. I am also very aware of the importance of calm, which is something I try to implement in my everyday routine.

As a reiki practitioner (reiki is a Japanese technique that uses energy – *rei* meaning universal, and *ki* meaning life energy – to promote relaxation, stress reduction and healing), I am able to pick up on the mood and energy of both people and dogs within a short time of being around them, and then adapt my own behaviour accordingly. This is something we can all tune in to with practice, and which will help in raising a happy, calm and fulfilled dog.

So as well as training, exercise and all things raising-a-dog related, we will also explore some how-tos, some mindful practices, exercises and quick tips to use both at home and when you are out walking with your dog. You will learn how to be in tune with them, looking at energy transfer, reiki, yoga with your dog and other relaxing meditative practices. Even something as simple as our music choices can impact a dog's mood, much as it does for us. Dogs are proven to reduce our blood pressure and release endorphins (feelgood chemicals), so including them in mindful pursuits is only going to heighten the experience and you can both enjoy this bonding time together. Taking time to practise mindfulness and be a calm and present dog guardian every day will improve your life and outlook – and, importantly, your dog's too. In short, you will become the zen master of dog guardians.

1

CHOOSING A DOG

I am sure you have heard this a thousand times before, but these wee souls are not just for Christmas or Hannukah or birthdays. Because the last thing anyone wants to see is yet another pair of eyes peering out of a rehoming centre's kennel.

Being the lucky new custodian of a dog is a huge responsibility, especially in the fast-paced world we live in, so it needs to be a well-thought-through decision, not just a whim and fancy. Although your dog will provide you with surges of endorphins, which will keep you youthful (forget the Botox!), they will also drive you bonkers with their naughty ways – my dogs' antics include chewing any child's toy left on the floor, chomping on dummies (probably not a bad thing, as my toddler is hooked on the things like a tiny addict), rolling in fox business and nibbling things like wretched moths; and even the best-behaved, best-trained dog will have days where they drive you to distraction. So you have to take the good with the bad and accept that even with the best will in the world, they have their own minds and will stretch the boundaries, test you, and get bored and possibly destructive. But the good, beautiful, heartwarming moments will outweigh the bad if you put the work in, especially in the beginning.

You are your dog's guardian, their protector, their caregiver and, as such, your job is to remain a constant in their life – and not just in the physical sense, in that you are present for their whole life, but also by understanding the importance of being consistent in your behaviour, too. Shouting and getting cross will have no positive impact on your dog; at all times, you need to be calm. Yes, you may need work on training in some areas, but this should always be a positive experience leading to positive results. So remember the three Cs: be a calm, consistent and confident guardian and your dog will respect you far more for it.

Your Lifestyle

There are so many things to consider when thinking about getting a dog. What if you have young children? No garden? Multiple pets? Do you enjoy running every morning or do you lounge around like a lizard on a sizzling rock? Do you have time to dedicate to a rescue dog? This is such a wonderful thing to do, giving them a second chance. And on this point, did you know that most breeds and cross breeds will have an associated charitable body who rehomes them, so it's a good idea to see if the perfect pooch is already waiting in a foster house for you. These dogs don't always come from painful situations, requiring lots of help and rehabilitation; sometimes they are made homeless due to a break-up, financial issues or a house move. Even show dogs can be moved on from a busy commercial kennel. There are so many scenarios through which dogs come up for adoption.

And it's not just about your situation right now. Think about how circumstances may change. What happens if you change jobs and find yourself out of the home all day, for example? There are ways of juggling your work and ensuring your pal isn't left alone for long periods, but you need to think about this in advance. You could use the services of a dog walker to take them out or do a home visit, you could book them into a doggy daycare centre to make friends and play or use a kennel facility that offers day boarding. You can also dog swap with one of your friends or family (you care for their dog and, in turn, they care for yours as a regular agreement. (Or what I do is phone my long-suffering mother for her dogsitting services!) You also need to think about what you will do when you want to go on holiday. And do you have someone to help with the dog if work calls you away for a week?

Do you have a garden or outdoor space? While this is ideal for anyone who is considering getting a dog, especially a puppy who needs lots of toilet breaks, it's not necessarily a deal breaker. As long as you're willing and able to put in the time and effort for walks, or arrange for someone else to do so (they should be walked regularly, even with a garden), you could still make it work.

Being aware of your situation, your needs and what you can offer a dog is a really great base from which to start your dog-searching adventure. And be patient – remember, all the best things in life are worth waiting for. I'm sure that for you – as for millions of others across the world – dog guardianship will be one of the best choices you'll ever make and, like most, once a dog guardian, always a dog guardian; but I want you to take some time to think things through, so that it's not just a knee-jerk decision. Again, a dog is not just for today, tomorrow and next year – it's for life.

The Right Dog for You

So, you have decided a dog is right for you and your situation; you have thought about your lifestyle and how a dog will fit into it. But what dog?

There are so many breeds and crosses – and they are each as different as we are. You probably already have your favourites. Maybe you like the big eyes, the long nose or the droopy ears that trail on the floor. We are all drawn to a specific aesthetic in a dog. But don't just pick your dog based on looks: don't choose the dog you have seen on Instagram wearing the cute-summer-hat-and-T-shirt combo – this dog and their temperament may be absolutely unsuitable for you and your lifestyle; and that pug you have been saving images of may not be right for your home. All too often, dogs are chosen on their appearance alone without consideration for the personality behind those eyes.

IMPORTANT LIFESTYLE CONSIDERATIONS AT A GLANCE

🐾 Does your work demand that you are out of the home a lot?

🐾 Is someone at home most of the time?

🐾 Do you have time in your life to dedicate to the needs of a dog?

🐾 What do you do in your spare time?

🐾 Do you have a settled home life and financial situation?

🐾 Who is living under your roof? Are there any small pets, other dogs or children?

🐾 How much experience do you have with dog guardianship?

You and your dog will become a partnership and, just like our life partners, the two of you have to be compatible, rubbing along together, working off the same energy levels – because you will be living together for over ten years, occupying the same sofa and enjoying shared activities.

An example of an incompatible pairing that springs to mind is a gentleman I see regularly. He is in his twilight years, walks with a stick and owns a young working Border Collie – a super brain in the dog world with strong instincts. The dog, now in a muzzle, drags the chap along dangerously, while trying to chase cars, spinning uncontrollably in frustration. If I'd had a chance to talk to the man before he decided to walk his Collie, I would have explained that it might have been more sensible to give one of the many older dogs in rescue centres a chance, as I'm not sure how his current pairing will safely continue.

Conversely, there's the lady I see who is nothing short of an athlete. She goes out running, while what looks like a pug cross, pants his head off as he struggles to keep up at the very end of the lead, that brachycephalic skull shape characteristic of flat-nosed breeds impeding his respiratory system. As she clearly enjoys exercise and being out with her dog, one built for running distances would have been so much more suitable. She could even have taken up canicross (cross-country running with dogs).

Incompatibility, as seen in the two examples above, is just setting yourself up for obstacle after obstacle, preventing you from gelling or understanding your dog. We have bred dogs in such an array of sizes, shapes, coat types, colours and to do various jobs for us humans, so getting the right one at the beginning and making it a mindful decision can help to reduce the number of rehome and rescue dogs we have sitting in our centres.

You may love the look and tenacity of a Lakeland Terrier, but what if you have an aged cat (I know some Terriers love living with other small animals but many don't). And what about if you love hillwalking, hiking – then a breed like a Bulldog probably isn't going to suit you (I'm sure there are exceptions, but generally speaking, they are lazy bums who won't enjoy that as much as you do – plus, they struggle to regulate their temperature due to their short noses).

A great place to start if you are unsure is somewhere like the Discover Dogs area at Crufts. There they host every breed of dog from the bearded Affenpinscher to the hairless Xoloitzcuintli. But if you can't make it there (or somewhere like it), do your research. There are online groups for different breeds and you can speak to experienced guardians who will spill the beans on the pros and cons of their breed. Mindful purchasing and homing are key – so stop, take a moment, breathe and make sure you really think things through.

Baby joy

Puppies are adorable, they are fun, smushie and cheeky. But they are also hard work, especially when it comes to moulding one to fit into our modern, busy, hectic lifestyle. If you have decided that the rescue route isn't for you and have your heart set on a pupster, then once you have followed the advice above to pin down the right breed or cross breed for you/your family, it's time to do some research on breeders. Only consider the good ones – those who love, care for and are dedicated to their chosen breed, their sole aim being to improve it to breed not only sound-tempered dogs but ones that are structurally beautiful, too. A good breeder will let you view Mummy and the whole litter and will carry out all the various health checks required for their breeding (you can find out about these online – see Resources, p. 248) and be able to show you the necessary paperwork relating to this.

At this point, you can use your instincts: do the pups all look healthy? (Are their eyes clear and bright? Do they have a decent amount of weight on them? They should be clean, with no signs of sore or dry skin. Are they bounding around, moving as you would expect on four strong legs? Do they engage with you and appear inquisitive? Are they all flea and parasite free with nice pink gums and white gnashers?) Does Mum look heathy and happy, too – a good weight and attentive to her pups? You really have to have your wits about you here because even puppy farms use 'staged homes', pretending to have bred the pups in their homes; they will even have the mothers of the dogs there, too, while keeping their puppy farming under wraps. So be sure to ask lots of questions (see box on page 16).

A caring breeder should ask you lots of questions, too. It can almost feel like an interview. But that's good – it means they are really bothered about where their precious cargo is going.

Often, breeders will put 'endorsements' on their dogs to prevent you breeding without their consent and a stipulation that if for whatever reason you can no longer take care of the dog, it has to be returned to them. These are good signs. It shows that they care about where the puppies are placed and want to make sure they aren't exploited. We can do so much to help eradicate and stop preventable diseases in our dogs through careful and considered breeding. Such preventable illnesses include parvovirus, canine distemper, leptospirosis, rabies (although not in the UK); and common preventable genetic diseases include hip and elbow dysplasia, luxating patella, brachycephalic syndrome, epilepsy, dilated cardiomyopathy, atopy/allergic dermatitis, Addison's disease, thyroid issues and progressive retinal atrophy (PRA).

QUESTIONS TO ASK BREEDERS

🐾 Will there be a contract of sale?

🐾 What should you feed the puppy and how often?

🐾 What are their exercise needs – and should this be limited until they are fully grown? (See p. 199 for more on this.)

🐾 Ask to see vaccine records and dates of previous and next worming doses.

🐾 Can you have a copy of a Kennel Club pedigree certificate if a pedigree dog?

🐾 Can they provide evidence that the required health tests have been carried out on both parents of the puppy, along with an explanation of the results and relevant information regarding any inherited diseases?

🐾 Be wary of any breeder who is unable or unwilling to answer these questions.

If you see a puppy in a bad situation, it can be really hard to walk away. But understand that by buying from a disreputable breeder you are perpetuating the supply and demand and the poor breeding bitches will just be subjected to more cycles of unethical breeding. Instead, report these unscrupulous people (in the UK to the RSPCA and the local authority or online – see Resources, p. 248; if you are overseas, look for a local authority, humane society or the police). Supply as much information as possible and know that as hard as it was to leave the puppy/ies behind, hopefully you will have caused something to change.

Often, quality breeders may not have many litters. This is where patience is key – because sometimes you have to wait for the right dog. I have had to wait a year for a dog before now. You can imagine, when the day came to pick her up I was like a dog with a bone! But it was worth the wait, and it also gave me time to get organised, research my breed, think of all the exciting things we were going to do together, daydream about beach walks and sitting by a pub fire together. It's nice to take that time to really make it a well-thought-through and mindful decision.

Rescue dogs

I think it's a great idea to stop by your local rescue centre before jumping into bed with the idea of a puppy from a breeder. Check them out; you just never know – the perfect soul might be there, destined for you to meet them that day. Talk to the staff because even if you are set on the idea of a puppy, they get puppies in, too. But keep an open mind – if you would consider an older dog, it's a beautiful thing to do. There are so many older dogs in our rescues, purely due to their age, and they would make wonderful companions, especially for someone older who doesn't want to embark on taking care of a youngster.

But even if you decide against the rescue route, see if you can help the charity in any other way. It may be a case of collecting bedding or food, giving a donation or helping with fund raising. I rarely walk past a charity stand without giving what I can. I'm a big believer in the idea that 'giving is receiving' – one good turn leads to another, and the sense of satisfaction you get from helping in even the smallest way is heartwarming.

Refugees

Another option to explore is a refugee from overseas. There are a lot of displaced dogs in kill shelters (facilities where homeless animals wait for adoption; but once they are full or a dog has been there over a certain length of time, they are euthanised) around the world and plenty of charities working with them, bringing them over to safety and for homing.

2

GETTING ORGANISED

Now that you have a new dog on the way, you need to get yourself and your home organised in order to create a zen-like space for both them and you. So ahead of the arrival of those four paws, give some thought to choices regarding the basics. My checklist before picking up a new dog would include the following:

- Food
- Bedding
- Crate (yes or no?)
- Toys and things to chew
- Walking paraphernalia
- Car accessories (car seat mat, travel harness)
- Worming treatments
- A designated vet practice
- Insurance
- Stair gates (if required)
- Secure garden
- Poop sacks

We will talk about all of these in the course of the book, but let's start with a look at food.

Food for Thought

What are you going to feed your dog? Do some research ahead of time and have the food of choice in place, ready. But also try to find out what the dog is currently fed on, as you will need to make a gradual change if you are altering their diet.

Here, in a nutshell, are the main food options and types (for more detailed information on food, see Chapter 7):

🐾 Grain-based dry kibble – clean and easy to feed, but not the most tempting or the highest in nutritional value

🐾 80/20 kibble – clean and easy to feed with a high nutritional content

🐾 Tinned meat – more tempting, but pretty stinky and not great for those gnashers

🐾 Raw – nutritionally high in value, tempting, free from preservatives; knowledge needed to ensure you are feeding a balanced diet (and lots of freezer space needed, too)

🐾 Pre-prepared raw – high nutritional value, pre-packed, balanced and convenient; freezer space required

🐾 Gently cooked – very tempting, balanced, high nutritional value (and it means you are not handling raw meat); freezer space required

🐾 Mixed feeding – mixes your favoured kibble with raw, tinned or gently cooked food

As you can see, with all these foods come varying degrees of nutritional quality – and price points, too. Try to avoid the cheapest foods and buy those you can afford with the highest nutritional content. Like us, our dogs are what they eat.

Home Sweet Home

Your home is a sanctuary – a place where you feel safe and comfortable; somewhere you can be yourself. It's your identity and a place for centring. And it's the place you always come back to. My home makes me happy, and it makes my dogs happy, too. It's our haven.

Outside . . .

Think about your outside space. Is it dog proof? You won't want to be streaking up and down your road in a mad panic in pursuit of a missing hound. Some dogs won't show any interest in breaking free, but some will find the smallest of escape routes from your garden and their curiosity will get the better of them. I've had female dogs mostly and I find they are home birds, not interested in exploring the neighbours' patches. On the other hand, my male dog digs for Australia, can find a break in the thickest of hedges and, like my very own Dora the Explorer, makes it his mission to try to wander outside his patch. So to avoid the hassle, the danger and the upset of a lost dog, Fort Knox that garden. Not just for their safety, but also to protect against dog theft – you don't want to be constantly standing on guard while they enjoy a sunny day in the garden. In fact, I've taken it to the next level with three bolted gates and cameras – but you know what? It gives me peace of mind, and what's more valuable than that?

Again, for their safety, research plants that are poisonous to dogs. Puppies love to chew on plants and explore, but there are lots that are toxic to them (both indoor and outdoor varieties).

. . . and inside

What about inside your home? If a puppy is moving in, get the house organised. Scan all the areas your dog will occupy. It's just not possible to watch them all the time; a busy household equals distractions. I can be making dinner with a toddler under one arm, as he's insisting on being carried (that's boys for you!), my daughter asking me a million 'why' questions, my husband rabbiting on a work call – all of which makes it just impossible to know what an inquisitive puppy is up to. Yes, I pride myself on my ability to be a multitasking mama and have eyes everywhere, but we all have our limits, don't we?

So what keeps me confident in the knowledge that everyone is safe are the lengths I go to to dog-proof my home – but in an aesthetically pleasing way. Here are some tips for you:

- If you have children, you will need to put their toys in baskets out of reach (we have a few dolls in 'doll hospital', missing limbs).

- Tidy away wires from games consoles, mobiles, laptop chargers and lamps.

- Make sure all shoes have a home and are cleared away under your stairs or in a safe, dog-free zone (we recently had one nibbled school shoe courtesy of our youngest pup – and school shoes aren't cheap).

- Have loads of interesting dog toys, showing them what's theirs to play with. And if your dog is gleefully carrying contraband, take it off them with a higher reward – a delish treat or their own favourite toy.

- My TVs are all wall-mounted, with no stray wires (those corner TV floor units with a spaghetti maze of wires are a real danger for cheeky, investigative pups).

- Ornaments should all be on shelves out of the way (the tails on some dogs mean that knick-knacks on coffee tables can get a battering).

- My bins are now integrated into my kitchen units – I know, fancy! – although you needn't go to the trouble of remodelling your kitchen (unless you were planning to anyway, in which case, honestly, it's a game changer!). But bored dogs can easily knock over and raid a flimsy bin. (My Miniature Poodle even managed to get into my mum's substantial and rather expensive touch-top bin, while my Dobermann used to tap it with her chin to open the lid, like her very own snack stand.) A bin can be such a dangerous place for a dog, what with bones, sharp packaging, poisonous foods (to dogs), plastic . . . you can imagine. So invest in a decent bin and think about what will work for you, especially when you are out – it can be too tempting for a dog to ignore a good old stinky bin when no one is watching.

- If your dog can get upstairs, use stair gates to limit their access (you can buy some ok-looking ones these days). The bathroom bin with all its tissues is a favourite spot for my pooches, so a gate is useful – even if you don't have stairs, and especially if you have an open-plan living space and want to limit your dog's access to certain rooms while they are settling in.

🐾 Heights can pose a real danger to pups, and they can be especially clumsy, so think in terms of having a toddler in the house and how you would limit opportunities for them to leap around from heights (see also p. 112).

🐾 As mentioned previously, be conscious of your house plants and flowers – some are both irritants and poisonous to dogs, so start regifting and replacing with safer options.

🐾 Move any precious rugs – believe me, those long, shaggy ones won't stand up well to puppy pee and poop and are a pig to clean.

Just taking the time to turn your house into a safe haven will not only give you a sense of relief and security but also means your precious new family member will be as safe as possible while they grow and change. Happy days all around.

Time for Sleep

Dogs should love their beds. (Crikey, I love mine and I'm pretty sure that lots of you love yours, too!) So just as it's so important for us to have a calm and welcoming space to retire to, your dog needs to feel the same way about their bed area.
Here are some of the options:

🐾 **Donut bed** Cosy and warm, and dogs often like the sides to rest on and bury themselves in. On the down-side, they are easily damaged, need washing regularly (and could be bigger than your washing machine), are not great in hot houses nor environmentally friendly.

- 🐾 **Plastic bed** These are durable and easy to clean, but not particularly pretty.

- 🐾 **Raised bed** Great for warm or cold climates, and for oldies or large breeds. And they are durable, too.

- 🐾 **Cushion bed** These have lots of padding for comfort and removable covers, which is a plus, but they are easily damaged by de-stuffers.

- 🐾 **Crate** Helps with house training and lots of dogs favour the den-style bed if introduced properly. You can fill them with any bed of your choice, but they are cumbersome and not particularly pretty.

- 🐾 **Vet-style bedding** Super hygienic, can be laid on top of anything, easy to clean, cosy and soft.

- 🐾 **Memory-foam bed** Excellent for comfort, especially with older dogs; but difficult to clean.

- 🐾 **Pet sofa** Looks great, but expensive and not easy to clean.

- 🐾 **Cave-style dog bed** A love-it-or-hate-it kind of thing, this is great for cold houses and short-coated dogs who like to hide.

- 🐾 **Blankets** Perfect for throwing over anything, easy to clean and you can pick them up at charity shops.

What bed does your dog like?

I have such an array of dog beds in my house that it's easy for me to work out which is each dog's preferred one.

In my utility, I've installed a dedicated dog-bed area under the counters with space for two crates, so my dogs can choose to sleep where they fancy – in the open crates or in the beds laid out (when they are puppies, I close the crates at night). This means the dogs have a cosy den to retire to that's both functional and aesthetically pleasing. Now that's next-level dog mamming!

I have always crate trained my dogs. In my experience, it's the easiest way. Find a nice, quiet corner for your dog's new crate bed (somewhere they can be away from the hustle and bustle, if they so wish), so they can relax, sleep and feel secure in the knowledge it's their zen den. As long as they are introduced to the crate in a slow and positive way (feeding them in the space, telling them 'in your bed' randomly through the day and rewarding with a delicious treat), they won't see it as an area of punishment or confinement or as a cage. When I want to get them used to sleeping or staying in the crate when I am heading out, it's a slow process, but once I know they are happy to sit in there with the door open, I start by sitting on the floor next to the crate when they are inside it and calm. Then I will move on to closing the door, then opening it and rewarding, gradually increasing the gaps between opening and closing the door. Then I work towards getting up and going into another room for only a minute and calmly returning. I don't make a big fuss – just quietly open the door.

You may notice a lot of this process is about being calm. Remember, this is a good state to be in for this type of training. As I will repeat frequently, dogs really do sense your behaviour and energy; they will pick up on your vibe if *you* get stressed out or frustrated if *they* get worked up about the crate. So if this happens, take it right back to the beginning, rewarding them in the crate with the door open or feeding them in there with the door shut but with you in sight before creating some space between you and them, so that they feel ok about you walking into another room briefly without feeling the need to jump up and follow you everywhere.

If you have seen a crate and think no way, it's a cage, try to switch up your mindset. It's a sanctuary – and you can always use covers to make it extra cosy if you want. In fact, even though I have dog beds all over the house (my husband rolls his eyes when I come home from a show with yet another one), my dogs choose their crates nine times out of ten over an open bed for sleep.

Where in the house should they sleep?

Once you have made a plan for *what* your new dog will sleep in, you need to think about *where* you will put them when they first come home.

There are several choices, the most common tending to be in the kitchen, with the run of the house, on the landing or in their bed. My feeling is that little ones shouldn't be locked away and ignored if they cry at night, and although there is a line where returning to them and worrying over them will make the problem worse, my sympathy does go out to the new dog when they have left their mother and/ or everything they have known and are moving into a new environment (especially without other dogs present).

Ultimately, however, whatever works for you and your dog is what you should opt for. Dogs like boundaries and structure, so with the right introductions and positive training (see p. 67), they will soon adjust. But even if you do opt to have them in your room, sleeping on your bed, you should still do crate training with them.

BEDMATES?

So your dog is now in your bedroom, on the bed, sharing your pillow, perhaps, or warming your toes. But was this your intention when you planned your doggy partnership? Or did they creep out of the kitchen, into the living room, on to the landing, do an SAS roll across your bedroom floor and before you knew it, they'd elbowed your partner out of bed? (You definitely have a Vizsla!)

Joking aside, it's much harder to take back steps – by which I mean that once your dog is fully wise to the comforts of Egyptian cotton and a king-sized bed, it's going to be difficult to get them back down into the kitchen. If it works for you and you prefer sharing your bed with your fuzz head, that's grand. Who cares? Your bed, your rules. But if it's likely to cause issues, and the nocturnal trumps are going to be too much to bear, I would reconsider that leap on to the bed. Once you taste the high life and all that . . .

My dogs have all settled pretty well and I attribute it to the fact that they have each other and they all co-sleep. So if a new puppy comes into the home, when they've been successfully introduced to the other dogs, I will try sleeping them with the others (but in a crate). They watch the older dogs and pick up on behaviours, so once they realise it's all good, they settle fast. Little ones learn so much from spending time with other dogs.

My dogs are not allowed upstairs, unless they are invited. It's our rule, because we don't want sixteen individual paws to have the run of the house. So I only let them upstairs sometimes, and only when I am there; they lie in my office with me and sometimes like to watch me get ready. But my house isn't a free for all. As we have seen post-lockdown with people no longer around 24/7, there's a separation-anxiety epidemic in our dogs, so it's not such a bad thing to make sure they feel settled away from us – that they can 'be' on their own. It's all about giving them the confidence to be ok with that.

Organising You

Your home is now looking like one hell of a zen dog den – safe and dog friendly with less chance of you getting anxious about your new arrival. Happy dog parent = happy dog.

Next, it's time to get your diary in order, ensuring you have that side of your life covered for the pending pooch. The last thing you need is a panic because you are due to be away for work with no dog care; or you have a holiday planned and no idea where they will go for theirs.

Regardless of whether you are getting a pup or an adult dog, you should take some time off work to settle them in. Find a good training and socialisation class to enrol them into (see box on p. 32). They should also be able to help you with recommendations for dog walkers, dog sitters, kennels and perhaps groomers. Us dog folk can be a chatty bunch and asking for recommendations is a great way of finding a suitable pet professional.

FINDING A PUPPY CLASS

Word of mouth is brilliant for finding a trainer who has been tried and tested. I also love the IMDT here in the UK (the Institute of Modern Dog Trainers) – they have a comprehensive list of modern dog trainers across the country, all working with kind, positive-reinforcement methods (see p. 40 for more on these methods and Resources, p. 248 for contact information).

Choices, choices

I feel that as long as I'm organised, I can deal with the busy-ness of a life juggling dogs, children and work and not be a complete stress head. A dog needs a calm guardian and for me, organisation helps me achieve the necessary balanced state of mind. So when you embark on your dog journey, get yourself organised ahead of time, too. Think about groomers, vets, walkers, insurance, worming, feeding, bedding, leads and any other paraphernalia you will need (e.g. dog toys).

On the subject of service providers, regardless of the type you choose, always ask about their experience and whether they have qualifications in their field. It's lovely to find one you are happy with and stick with them, and it's so important for your dog, too, as they will build a rapport with them, feeling more comfortable, settled and confident. Chopping and changing between walkers, groomers and daycare services isn't great for your dog's confidence. Like so many of us, they like routine and familiarity.

With so much choice when it comes to service providers and equipment, here is a little guidance to point you in the right direction:

🐾 **Groomers** I love word of mouth – if you see a dog with a nice haircut, ask their guardian where they go (the dog, that is; unless you need a hairdresser for yourself, too). You can also try a website called The Groomers Spotlight (see Resources, p. 248) to find fully qualified groomers in your area. And remember to repeat book when you pick your dog up, as good groomers get booked up quickly.

🐾 **Walkers/daycare** If you see a lovely walker out enjoying time with a small, controlled pack of dogs, ask for their details – maybe they could take on your pal. Or maybe daycare would suit you if you're stuck out all day. Find a suitable facility by asking friends, your vet, your dog walker – anyone who might have first-hand experience in using one. Forums and social media pages are also a great tool for seeking out these services. Once you have found one that seems to fit the bill, pop in there for a visit. See if they are ok with 'as-and-when' bookings, as well as fixed days, then get your dog enrolled. They should want to see vaccination certificates or titre test results (a blood test that determines the levels of antibodies in the dog's bloodstream).

🐾 **Pet-care providers** If you are likely to go away without your dog, seek out a pet-care provider early; don't leave it too late, especially during busy times like school holidays. Again, ask your vet/groomer/walker/ friends for recommendations. Make sure that you ask for references and checks and that *they* ask *you* all the questions you would expect about your dog (about vaccination status, for example – see box p. 45).

🐾 **Kennels** These are generally safe places to leave your dog. Many are modern and heated and don't mix the dogs much, which is good for the more reserved and less sociable types. They will ensure your dog has clean water and is regularly fed. However, the downside to kennelling is that it can be a shock to the system for many a pampered pooch, especially when they are used to a lot of human contact and sleeping on your bed, for example. If you are happy to use a kennel, there are some decent ones out there, but also some I personally wouldn't be happy leaving my dogs in. The best way of finding a good one is, again, through a recommendation, so ask your vet/groomer/walker if they have ever used one or have a search online. Then visit them and see what you think – is this somewhere your dog will settle and enjoy a holiday, too? Make sure the staff are friendly and happy to show you around, ensure there is clean water down in each kennel, the environment is clean and that the dogs have adequate bedding areas. Check that it's warm in winter and well ventilated and that the dogs have space to run and stretch their legs.

🐾 **Vets** Choosing a vet pretty close to you is, I feel, a must. Dogs get up to all sorts of mischief and you don't want to be driving miles across a busy town during peak traffic to get to your vet in an emergency. A lot of vets in my area don't have a 24/7 facility, but they partner up with other practices to share night shifts or to deal with out-of-hours cases. Keep a note of opening times and locations and have the numbers saved in your mobile for speed dialling.

🐾 **Insurance** A new pup may come with four weeks' free insurance from their breeder but find out about this prior to collection, so you can have a policy set up just in case. There are so many pet-insurance companies out there now, and the best way to find out about good ones is by asking at your vet's practice – they deal with them all the time and will be able to help you with this.

Some insurance companies will insist that you pay the vet bills yourself and then claim back the money from them; others will pay the vets directly. Depending on your financial situation, it may be worth knowing this sort of detail before signing up to one. Comparison websites can also be useful when it comes to finding the best deal, as there are so many different cover options and prices. My advice to you is to always go for a lifetime policy for your dog – this means that should they develop an illness that is ongoing for several years or even their whole life, the insurers will continually pay out for it, not just as a one-off.

🐾 **Worming** There are many types of worms found in dogs – roundworms, hookworms (not common in the UK), tapeworms, whipworms, lungworms and heartworms. It's important as the custodians of our dogs that we look after them internally, as well as caring for their diets and mental health. Dogs should generally be wormed every month up to the age of six months and then every three months thereafter but speak to your vet for their recommendations. (If your dog is particularly partial to a carcass, you should mention this to your vet in case they advise you to worm more frequently.) Puppies should be regularly wormed by their breeder from when they are tiny up until when you collect them, after which you can take over.

🐾 **Identification** Although your dog should be micro-chipped (a small chip is inserted under their skin by the vet, which, when scanned, shows your details), they should also wear a collar when out of the home with a tag attached bearing your contact details and any medical-emergency information. This way, if the worst happens and the dog goes missing, you can be easily contacted.

🐾 **Collars and harnesses** I like a rolled collar for longer-coated dogs, but just make sure you buy one that's appropriate for your dog's size. I personally hate big, stiff buckles and difficult fixings, preferring an easy clip fastening or easily manipulated buckle. The collar shouldn't be so tight as to be uncomfortable but also not so loose that it just slips over their head. I use the two-finger test: ensure you can get your middle and index fingers underneath the collar. Depending on the breed of your dog and their skull shape, this should be sufficient as a gauge (except with greyhound- and whippet-type dogs, whose skulls are the same size as their necks, so this rule doesn't really work for them).

You may prefer to use a harness on your puppy because when they are young and they are pulling around a lot, collars can put pressure on their trachea as they lunge forwards and cause them to cough and choke. Ultimately, the collar-vs-harness debate is about what suits you and your dog. You may embark on lead training from day one and work closely with the dog, so no harness is ever needed.

Harnesses are great for using in the car if they sit in the rear seats. You can get specialist car harnesses for safe travelling and they are good for dogs who pull a lot, but they must be fitted correctly, so they don't interfere with their movements or rub them under their armpits – ask at your pet shop for advice on the correct fitting. I do like to use a collar and lead on my trained dogs; they aren't on the lead often, though, preferring to roam wild and sniff all the sniffs to be sniffed.

Leads There are training leads, retractable leads, thin leads, rope leads, long lines – start with a normal-length, lightweight lead and wait to see what your trainer recommends for recall work. Personally, I'm not a fan of retractable leads. I find them really cumbersome and even dangerous if used near a road. I've heard too many horror stories to make me comfortable using one. Long lines are fabulous for giving a dog in training freedom and are the lead of choice for many professional trainers, but they are a pain in the rear to carry and clean. Training leads are a good choice for training in and around home, as the length can be changed, but they aren't very long.

Toys Puppies love to play, so I recommend you make the most of this bonding opportunity by getting a selection of toys, each of which has its own particular job, as outlined next.

Toys for your pooch

Chew toys You can get nylon bones, KONGs and gummy keys – my pups love these. They relieve the dog from the discomfort of teething, which happens around three to seven months of age, but also offer a mental activity for them when they are bored. Dogs explore the world through their mouths and having access to these toys means your chair legs should remain intact. Chew toys like the KONG can also be stuffed with dog-friendly peanut butter or cream cheese and even frozen for that added soothing factor on the gums.

- **Balls** Dogs love to chase (a lot of them also have that herding instinct) and it's so much fun to build on your bond with them through playing together and reinforcing commands, such as 'Come' and 'Drop it'. Just ensure the ball isn't so small that the dog can choke on it.

- **Tug toys** Another lovely, interactive toy. If I'm too busy to play, the puppy will instigate a game of tug with one of my other dogs, and it's lovely to see how the older dogs play so gently with the younger, smaller ones. You can use the tug toy as a response to great behaviour, rewarding with a game instead of a treat. Just be careful those younger dogs don't get too exuberant and hurt themselves (see p. 112).

- **Puzzle toys** These offer fabulous mental stimulation; they really do work the mind and require the dog to think. Puzzle toys have treats inside them and the dog has to work out how to get at them. Dogs are super smart and there are loads of these on the market for varying degrees of intelligence, from the simpler puppy ones to the super-complex board games with sliders and removable lids.

- **Squeakers** These may be annoying to some, but in my house the squeak doesn't last long! These toys really bring out a dog's natural instinct – they will rag them, pounce on them and, in my dogs' case, destroy them in search of that squeak. I love the stuffing-free ones, as they last longer and have loads of different textures, which are great for your dog's senses – crinkly, crunchy, nobbly. Heaven.

Now you have all your ducks in a row, with all bases covered for any eventuality. And that, in turn, equals less stress, a smashing life and ten doggy parent points to you!

Setting Boundaries

You are about to em-bark (woof) on a new journey with your puppy or adult dog, so it's time to make some house rules. Setting boundaries for your new family member is important, even when it comes to jumping up. Make sure everyone (including visitors) knows the drill on acceptable behaviour to prevent chaotic training. I would say this needs to involve a proper family conversation – one where everyone is listened to and taken into account – because getting a dog is a big deal and you all have to cohabit in harmony.

We will look at training in more detail in Chapter 4, but in the meantime, here are some points to consider when setting boundaries:

🐾 **Will your dog be allowed upstairs?** My husband is a no-to-upstairs person, and I respect that; and (for the most part – except for when I sneak them up if they're clean and dry) I also prefer it that way. If we had one or maybe two dogs, they would be allowed upstairs, but with so many tiny feet charging around the house, it makes sense that keeping that space dog free means less mess and chaos. Also, my children have toys all over their bedrooms that, for my young dogs, make excellent chew toys. We also have quite a few bedroom/ bathroom bins that my oldie likes to raid (her particular favourite is a snotty tissue or ear bud, but everything in those bins is fair game to that greedy missus). So keeping them downstairs is a safety concern, too.

POSITIVE TRAINING

When you think about your boundaries, you should be thinking about how you would implement them, and this is best done through positive training, or positive reinforcement.

Positive reinforcement is marking and rewarding a behaviour that you like to see and ignoring the rest. Your dog soon realises that if they do 'this' they get rewarded for it, and it becomes a default behaviour. You can train positively using food, praise, toys and play. Science tells us that this is the best way for a puppy to learn because it is fun, kind and really helps to build that trusting bond between the two of you. Positive training also helps dogs to use their brains and to think for themselves, using problem solving. Your timing has to be spot on, so using a marker word like 'Good' or a clicker (a small device with a button that, when pressed, makes a 'clicking' sound) really helps the puppy to pinpoint the behaviour they get a reward for.

🐾 **Nuisance barking** This is neither very neighbourly nor a relaxed and calm state for your dog. For me, it's fine for the dogs to let me know if someone is at the house, in my driveway or knocking at my door. The boundary I set here is when I say to them, 'Ok, I've got it' – when they have had their barking fun and it's enough. I don't want them to keep barking on and on and on. If they don't listen to me, I use distraction to stop them and find that teaching them to 'speak' (see p. 75) and to be 'quiet', using rewards for moments of calm and redirecting them to their beds really helps them to understand. And I am consistent. Of course, the cheeky devils will now and again go on and on – they are gobby poodles, after all, and when one goes they all go. This training has worked well in my house, where there is a pack of dogs whose breed is known for being noisy. However, it's also down to the dogs' confidence – if they feel safe, secure and mentally fulfilled, you will find there is a lot less noise. (What doesn't help is my dad, whose favourite sport is winding my dogs up, razzing them into a frenzy on purpose, just for the funnies!)

🐾 **Furniture** Should the dog be allowed to go on your furniture? Sofa, no sofa or a compromise: sofa when they are invited up, but they're not allowed to sit up there all day like a sloth.

🐾 **Greetings** I remember when people who loved a big dog met my first Dobermann I would say 'Pleaseeee don't let her jump up at you – just turn your back on her and ignore her,' but they would say 'Awwww, I love big dogs, I don't mind,' and proceed to tickle her ears, as she crawled up their jumpers, undoing all my work training her to keep her four paws on the floor for greetings. With the four small dogs I have now, I have a similar problem with well-meaning dog walkers with pockets full of dog biscuits, free-rein feeding them without my consent as the dogs jump all over them to get more biscuits.

🐾 **Begging** Will you allow the dog to roam around the table at dinner time, potentially begging or being fed on the sly by children? (I was a horror as a child when it came to this; we had a strict clean-plate-or-no-pudding rule growing up and I remember being ever so discreet as I directed my unwanted dinner under the table.) It's your dog, so you do you, but be clear what the house rules are so everyone is reading from the same hymn book.

🐾 **Mealtimes** Do you want them to sit in their beds during mealtimes? Would you put them in another room? Or perhaps you'd pull them up a chair? Again, it's about personal preference. We don't feed our dogs from the table at all (at least, not purposefully; but like little swarming sharks they will circle my children because they know where the good stuff comes falling down). They will eat anything, too, so, for safety, I put my dogs in another room. It's just easier than constantly telling them to sit in their beds, especially my old lady who has selective hearing and, like a scavenger, just can't help herself. They know the routine, it's consistent and they will get a titbit for going into the other room. And by now they pre-empt it – they know when dinner is being served and will wait for their treat for staying out of the room. My Dobermann used to sit in her bed in the dining room, but you would look over at the poor soul with the biggest slobber strings hanging out of her mouth, like she was chewing on a trainer! It was better for her stress levels that she didn't watch us eat. I remember tearing my hair out at first; I thought she would never get it. But with calm consistency and the boundaries you have set, it will happen. Positive training (see p. 67) takes time, but it's the right way. All that being said, some people are fine with having a dog hanging around their table.

As a rule, it's a lot easier to start off with more boundaries and then to relax them than it is to start with none and then try to implement some when the dog has settled in. What is unnerving for the dog is when they don't know what is ok and what isn't – for example, if one day the sofa is ok, and the next day it's off limits.

How it all goes wrong in my house is understanding that, at the end of the day, dogs will do cheeky things, even though they know they shouldn't. They are sentient animals, they have their own minds and they are not robots. Dogs will be dogs, so there may be the odd accident, there may be a decapitated Barbie here and there, there may be bin raids and holes in your gorgeous lawn, but you'll need to accept that all this is part and parcel of owning these creatures with their magnificent and individual personalities. My oldie, who's over twelve, knows she isn't allowed on the dining-room table (actually *on* the table), but if I ever leave food up there and have to quickly whizz the children into the bath, forgetting to clear their dinner plates, the old dear will be on that kitchen table quicker than anything! She'll hoover up all the leftovers, joined by my ten-month-old puppy, like a sneaky duo.

I'm house proud and like my house to be clean and tidy, but leaves, twigs and garden debris are trailed in every day and my expensive sofa has a nibble hole in it (now covered by a well-positioned throw), courtesy of my Toy Poodle when she was a baby. But I accept this and, believe me, the ups are well worth the bin juice all over the floor (although, now that we have an integrated bin, I have won that particular war).

I joke that Lily, my old girl, knows what's right and wrong, but she thinks doing the wrong thing is worth a tut because she's a Labrador in a curly body – that's just her – and where food is concerned, it's my fault for leaving it around. My Olive, on the other hand, spends every waking moment trying to make sure she has pleased me, looking up at me for a 'Who's a good girl?' That's just the way she is, too.

They are all so different. Even within the same breed, while they share certain traits, they have individual personalities and finding them and getting to know them is so exciting. From experience, you can get trickier and easier dogs – you just never know. And it's how you react to and deal with the micro-crises that makes you the zen master of dogs and a trusted dog guardian. Ultimately, though, if you think, Oh, man, I love my lawn too much – perhaps you should opt for a fish tank instead of Fido.

A WORD ON VACCINATIONS

Vaccination requirements vary enormously from place to place and dog to dog. But as a very rough guide, a recommended schedule might look a little like this:

At eight weeks
Infectious hepatitis
Distemper
Canine Parvovirus
Leptospirosis

At twelve weeks
Infectious hepatitis
Distemper
Canine Parvovirus
Kennel cough (for the more social dog)
Rabies (country dependent)

At one year
Infectious hepatitis
Distemper

Caine Parvovirus
Leptospirosis
Kennel cough (as above)

At two years
Leptospirosis
Kennel cough (as above)

At three years
Leptospirosis
Kennel cough (as above)
Rabies (as above)

At four years
Infectious hepatitis
Distemper
Canine Parvovirus
Kennel cough (as above)

Vaccinations will be carried out by a vet, and you will have a record of these to keep, should you wish to use a boarding kennel or daycare facility, for instance. If you decide to skip any vaccinations, be aware that this might invalidate your pet-insurance policy.

3

COMMUNICATION – UNDERSTANDING DOG

Dogs are all seeing and all knowing, so make no bones (excellent unprepared pun there), they will be watching you! Therefore, before we set about implementing training, it's important to look at how a dog communicates, both with their own species and also with humans.

Over time, we humans have evolved to rely very heavily on speech as a means of communication. But think about when you are on your jollies and trying to communicate in a foreign language – you may gesticulate a lot, wave your hands about and use facial expressions more. You become more dog-like, using a universal language without words.

We are much more aware now than even twenty years ago of how important it is to have a happy and calm dog, and that we don't 'own' them – we are merely the custodians of these intelligent, insightful creatures who should be treated with respect and kindness. They are sentient beings, aware of themselves and with the capability to feel joy, as well as pain and suffering. Having them in our lives should be regarded as both a blessing and a joy, but they do need training – to understand our strange habits, and what we want from them. And we must also appreciate that while we are trying to understand them, they are also trying to communicate with and understand us at the same time.

Dogs have a complex and vast array of communicative signals they use, via their body language, sense of smell, tail carriage and even their poop and pee. Understanding a dog's body language and behaviour throughout their life, from babyhood to their twilight years, will really help you to become a better and more aware dog custodian, whether you are out on a walk, assessing the behaviour of an oncoming dog, or just at home and your dog is behaving differently.

Body Language Basics

By studying your own dog and others', you get to interpret their cues and any small changes, which may signal a lot.

A relaxed dog

A relaxed dog will have a relaxed posture. Think of this as the neutral gear on your car – the one your dog should always return to after running rings around your kitchen. In this mode, your dog has a calm, downward-pointing tail, not between their legs but relaxed down and either gently swaying with a wag or not. Their ears, too, are relaxed, not pricked forwards on alert or swept back in worry. Their weight is calmly distributed over all four paws and they are neither up on their toes, ready to go, nor hunkering back. Finally, their face is neutral and their eyes may be blinking ever so slowly up at you (little treasure). That feeling you get lying in a warm bath after a busy day? That's what the dog is channelling.

A nervous dog

They may crouch down, turn their head away and draw their ears back. They may lift a leg off the ground and lick their lips or yawn in anxiety. They may be shivering and/or whining, with their tail firmly between their legs. Their eyes may be wide and focused on what's upsetting them.

A playful dog

Here comes the play bow: bum up, front down, tail held high and wagging, maybe even barking, instigating play. Their eyes are alert and all sparkly and their mouth may be open, tongue out, yipping with delight. Their ears can be neutral or pricked forwards in interest. When my dogs are being uber silly, they will do a wag involving their whole bum and their ears pulled back before bouncing off to find me their favourite toy.

A watchful, alert dog

Something has piqued their interest and they are on the lookout. What is it? It could be positive or negative, but they are sussing out the sitch. This mode is normally a pathway from one behaviour to another because something has caught their attention. Think of it as a change of gear. They will be stiffer in stance and almost leaning forwards; their tail will be straighter and carried up, even wagging. Their mouth will be closed and their ears pricked, as they concentrate on what's happening. Their eyes will be fixed in the direction of their wonder.

On the defence

Your dog feels threatened and unsure where to escape to, so they go on the defence, not wanting to attack, but feeling cornered. Now on the defence, they are back on their haunches, cowering, hackles up (that's when the hair over their shoulders and down their spine stands to attention, like a hedgehog). Their tail is tucked between their legs. Their ears are back and tucked into their head, their eyes are dilated and they may not want to look at what they are afraid of, so their head may be turned away slightly and they may be growling and showing their teeth.

On the offence

This is full offensive mode, on the attack, and is where you really need to step in and defuse the situation for the sake of all parties. The dog is standing strong on all four feet, leaning forwards towards the object of interest (almost pointing at it with their whole body), tail like a poker, bristled with anger, teeth bared and making direct eye contact with their point of interest. Not a happy place for any party involved.

Understanding Changes in Behaviour

Of course, dogs are individuals – like us – so there may be slight variations in these different forms of body language. For instance, with big pendulum ears it's harder to notice changes in their position, but instead you may notice a furrowed brow as they wrinkle up their face in interest.

It's also worth considering the breed or mix of breeds that you have. Take the Collie: they have a natural instinct to herd. In the past I've walked my dogs where a man walks his Collie. I have small dogs, like a little herd of woolly black poodle-sheep, and this Collie immediately clocks them and adopts the herding stance. It has all the instincts of a working dog, staring down my dogs, giving them that direct eye contact, and I can see straight away that my little pack look anxious – their tails go down, they keep checking and checking behind them and gather around me. The Collie then starts stalking towards them, prowling like a prairie dog, and, sensing the change in the air, I have to pop my dogs back on their leads and calmly leave the area in a nonchalant but timely manner. The Collie is just following its instinct here – the problem lies with its custodian, who is oblivious to the fact that his dog is coming across as a threat to other dogs and makes no effort to call it away and engage it in play or keep it in his space. In such cases, it's up to you to pre-empt a situation by just reading the body language of your own dogs and those around you.

Another example is when I was out walking my pack and I came across two ladies with their sighthounds – two lurcher types, off the lead. They seemed young and happy enough, frolicking around with each other, running in tandem. I gave them good space and passed with my dogs off the lead also. The lurchers then showed an interest in my dogs and, benign as they are, they were side glancing, walking away and not wanting to interact. Then the hounds started to chase one of my dogs, who got freaked and started running. I mean really running – that tail-tucked-between-the-legs, scooting-her-bum-under, wide-eyed-and-panicked kind of run. She was not enjoying this game of chase and was frightened. I quickly looked around to see the ladies simply continuing their chat. I tried calling my dog, but she was too frightened and being hotly pursued by two much, much larger dogs. She started crying out as she ran her little legs off.

The women were still oblivious, still chatting. I shouted to them to call their dogs back, but their response was that they were just playing with my dog and 'What's the problem?' If they'd understood anything about body language, they would have known it wasn't fun at all. It was a game of catch, my small poodle being the target – and while usually a placid little lady, she was now freaking the hell out.

I then had to shout at the women, pretty cross now, 'Can you not see they are frightening my dog?' She was now just running and running, that flight mode in full swing. In her mind, she was running for her life. Imagine if there had been a road nearby. If these ladies had understood their breed's traits and understood dogs' body language, they would have seen clearly that for my dog, this game of chase was not fun.

Dogs are acutely aware of their surroundings. They can pick up on the body language of another dog or a person across a field, before we, their custodians, have had a chance to even notice them. They have honed senses. That's why, on a walk, we should not only enjoy the surroundings, getting some exercise, but also be reading our dog's behaviour. It should be a second-nature thing: 'What is that dog thinking?'

I love my dogs to mix, play with and make new dog friends. Those moments when you see your dog just click with another – finding that one who is riding the same wave as them – are so joyful. But it can be a gamble. Sometimes, as I've described, inner chase, guard or herd instincts will kick in and it's up to you, as your dog's guardian, to be aware of this, with the necessary training to keep the situation safe and under control. Take the delightfully mischievous Beagle, for example. This was my husband's first dog and his family battled hard with that Beagle instinct to follow a scent. The dog would always selectively hear their recall and disappear off after something delicious-smelling. Or the Dobermann – such a loyal and intelligent dog, but one with a natural guarding instinct and a tendency to be stubborn.

A dog's inner instinct can be trained to really work for

us, but it is important for us as their caregivers to understand that it can be a case of balancing nature and nurture. By studying your dog, understanding the basics and always remembering they are animals with animal instincts, you'll have the knowhow to be a top dog communicator.

Your Dog's Brain at Work

To understand a dog, we need to think like a dog. But how *do* dogs think? That's a tricky one but, luckily, we have incredible scientists who have researched this.

It is thought that dogs have the cognition of a three-to-five-year-old. (Man alive – that means, counting all the young humans and dogs in my house, I'm living with six preschoolers. No wonder my days are so hectic!) The dog's brain has some similarities to the human brain, but is smaller; whereas our brain-to-body ratio is 1:40, a dog's is 1:125. That means that although they don't have as much brain power as we do, as animals they are very intelligent.

Dogs have minds of their own and personalities, and they experience a range of emotions we can understand. It is thought that a dog's brain is similar to a human's because we've evolved together so closely.

A dog's ability to solve a problem at speed has been shown to be something they have inherited from their wild ancestors. Dogs have similar chemical changes in their brains to humans, one of which is the release of oxytocin, the 'love hormone', which creates a sense of affection and love in the dog. Dogs also have thoughts in their heads like we do. Just *what* they are thinking, no one knows, but scientists do know that they are thinking about something . . . bones? Walks? Cuddles? And while they don't think in language or with symbols like we do, they can definitely be taught to recognise words and symbols.

Research has revealed that a dog's brain lights up when they are shown the cue for a reward (this is the same area of the brain that lights up in humans when we see something we really like). This is further evidence that positive reward-based training really does have a good effect on your dog.

Although smell is the primary sense for a dog, they also recognise people's faces and our different expressions, reading our micro-movements as a guide for their behaviour. One of my clients once left a picture of herself smiling on the table for her dog to look at while I was grooming it; this was many years ago and, at the time, I thought it was quirky, to say the least. But it looks like she was actually on to something!

Although we can't read their minds, we can read their body language, which is why understanding the big statements and micro-movements they make with their faces and bodies can mean that we have a better understanding of what is going through their minds.

We also know that dogs have feelings. They can actually feel anxiety, depression, fear, jealousy, happiness and optimism. They even respond in the same way as the human brain to antidepressants. That makes you stop and think how important your role as guardian is – not only looking after them physically with exercise, nutritious food and veterinary care when needed, but also feeding their minds, with love and understanding. Their characters, their inner selves can really be affected by how we treat them.

How to Communicate

What do dogs hear when we are talking? Well, most of our words are gobbledygook to them (although they do understand over 150 of them). Instead, they will be tuning in to our body language, facial expressions, pitch, tone of voice and smell. So it's not so much *what* we say to a dog that matters (which is just as well, given the number of times I lovingly tell my dogs they stink), but how we say it.

I have different voices for different occasions. When we are out on a walk, having fun, I'm animated, speaking louder than my 'inside' voice, engaging and joyful. Then there's my around-the-house voice, which is calm, fairly quiet and relaxed. I have my training voice, too, which is clear, focused and free from chitchat, while still calm. And, finally, there's my dog voice – a special one I use when I'm pretending the dog is talking back to me; it's an oooshie-whoooshie kind of voice that varies, depending on the dog's character.

Understanding body language and how a relaxed shoulder, a kind eye and a calm heart rate can convey so much more than words to your dog is a great base for learning how best to communicate with them, so that they will gravitate towards your wonderful energy.

Like a mirror, dogs will pick up on and imitate your behaviour and energy levels. Often, I'll notice the mirroring of behaviours, when a hyped-up guardian is trying to regain some level of control over a wayward hound, but their energy is all wrong and it comes across as a game. Or I've had custodians come and collect their dogs from daycare and be super-excited to see them; their voices go up and they speak super-fast, so the dog is razzed up, comes tearing out, leaping at them and mouthing them. Then a second later, they do a U-turn and start telling the dog off, 'Get down; stop it; it's too much'. This is so confusing for a dog. In that nano-second, with that shift of gear energy-wise, they forget the boundaries you've set.

I'm always wittering on to my dogs, chatting to them as companions. They are used to this, and my Dobermann in particular was amazing at deciphering my monologues and hearing key parts of what I was saying. But when you are out, for instance, and you want your dog to come back to you, that's not the time to be waffling on at them in the way you might do in your garden. You need to make sure your communication is calm, clear and positive, saying their name just the once, and issuing a clear command: come!

Sign language

Another way that we can communicate with a dog is through hand gestures. Dogs are very good at learning a sign for a command, the most common being to raise your forearm at the elbow, bringing your hand up towards your face (as if you're guiding a plane on to a runway), as you ask a dog to sit. This is a useful tool and is no more difficult than teaching them verbally. Plus, it's great for communicating with them over a distance.

Just about everything you teach a dog with a verbal cue can be taught using a hand signal:

- 🐾 To ask the dog to lie down, you move your hand in front of your body and motion to push down.

- 🐾 To stop barking, give the shhh signal over your mouth.

- 🐾 To encourage the dog to make eye contact, point to the side of your eye.

- 🐾 To get them to roll over, use your index finger to motion a circle in front of your body.

- 🐾 For a spin, bring your arm out and motion a circle again, but in the direction of the ground.

- 🐾 For a jump, raise your hand up above your body.

🐾 For a high five, crouch and put your hand out for that five – similar to the stay (where you stand up straight and hold your palm out in front of you, like a halt or stop sign).

🐾 To ask the dog to come, bring your hand in to your chest.

I signal to my dogs by pointing a lot, too, so they have learned to follow a point. I did this initially by placing a treat on the ground at close proximity and pointing to it, then gradually moving away. With the dogs' amazing problem-solving brains, they realise the point is me showing them something to look at and go towards. It's super helpful when, for example, I am in mid-conversation with someone and just need to indicate something to my dog, or for them to go outside, or to help them find a ball in a field (they look to me for a point in the right direction). These signs can be anything you want them to be – they don't have to be the most widely recognised signals.

Eye contact

It's a must in my book that you have a strong connection with your dog, and this can be reinforced with some good old, non-awkward eye contact. It's such a treat to have those glassy peepers staring up at you, saying, 'Come on, then – what's next?' Train your pal to 'look at me' – I do this with a bribe, normally in roast-chicken form. I bring it right up to my eyes, ask the dog to look at me and, as soon as that eye contact is made, I quickly give the reward. I keep practising by moving my hand away from my face and using the cue 'look at me', and, if they shift their gaze from the food and into my eyes, I mark that behaviour quickly with a 'yes' and reward. This is a great one to have in your arsenal for when the dog needs some redirected attention and for training, also for that look of love and burst of endorphins after a stressful day.

Facial expressions

Did you know that dogs can even read our facial expressions? They watch for micro-movements on our faces that may give away nervousness, apprehension, tension and glee – all across the spectrum – and they can read moods and our energy. It's a great reason why we should practise deep breathing and relaxation techniques when we are feeling the weight of the world. Because how we feel can have a

COMMUNICATING TO MARK BEHAVIOUR

To reinforce the behaviour you want to see, you need to 'mark' it. It's a bit like putting a pin in it, so the dog understands that what they just did there was exactly what you wanted them to do. You can use a clicker for this, a marker word or both.

It's helpful to train your dogs to understand both a clicker and a marker word as you won't always have a clicker to hand. Verbal cues like 'yes' or 'good' work well, as they are one syllable. To mark a behaviour, you would click or give your verbal mark and reward as quickly as possible. You don't want to be fumbling around for a bit of sausage, so get yourself a treat pouch and aim to reward within three seconds. If you are slow at getting that reward into their postbox, it may confuse and distract them from your training session.

direct impact on our canine companions. That's probably why they make such excellent therapy animals – why when we are feeling blue, they come along with the big, delicious snugs we need, and, when we are feeling excited, they have energy to match. So it's worth noting that what we put into a dog is what we get out of them; a positive and balanced mindset really will have a kinetic effect upon your dog.

Communication and Age

Does the way we communicate have to evolve and change as the dog grows and ages? I think so, absolutely. Think of it like parenting: you wouldn't communicate with your baby or toddler in the same way as you would with your granny. And I believe the same applies to dogs. As they grow, their wants and needs alter, too.

The energy I bring to the table shifts, depending on the behaviour I want to see from my dog and how they are acting. To calm a bouncing dog on a quiet evening, try stimulating their minds with some quiet play, such as a puzzle, and let them feel your relaxed energy. Conversely, when my oldie is being a slug in her bed, I bring a higher energy when I am communicating with her, enticing her to play and pulling out my rainy-day basket of toys, which never fails to interest.

With older dogs, they know their routine and can really understand your communication, so you have a much better understanding of each other's quirks.

Being in Tune With Your Dog's Needs

They grow up so fast. One minute you are excitedly taking your puppa on their first car journey, bringing them home; the next, they are wearing their big-boy boots and enjoying

Mindful tip

Mindful communication means understanding and having an awareness of your own emotional state and your dog's, too.

When you are communicating with your dog, clear away all the head chatter and focus on *what* you are communicating. Be patient and ensure that every interaction is a positive one. Think about how you are holding yourself and relax and smile. Try plastering a smile on your face right now and see how you feel. This increases levels of serotonin and dopamine in your body, so tricking your brain into feeling happier and lifting your mood (I just did it, and laughed at myself!).

long walks with you as a fully grown dog. Then, like a flash, some grey whiskers appear on their chin and they are getting older. And as they do so, they mature, they change. Being in tune with your dog is something you should work on through all these stages, throughout their life. As previously, taking the time to read their body language and behaviour will give you an insight into how they may be feeling and what are they thinking.

Having said that, often when something is right under your nose it's harder to notice the subtle changes that take place over time. Sometimes, as dog groomers, it's easier for us to spot these things when we see a dog maybe only once every couple of months. Looking at coat condition and mobility, we will often notice a decline sooner than you would at home. I have lost count of the number of conversations I've had with custodians over their dogs' declining mobility and possible arthritis. And while I cannot diagnose a problem as I am not a vet, I can raise concerns, and, in the course of a chat with a dog's custodian, asking how they are getting on at home, it might emerge that they have noticed, say, increased licking of the legs and an unwillingness to walk as much (basically joint pain, which has been interpreted as stubbornness) or spending more time in bed (pain and depression, interpreted as laziness). With a quick trip to the vet, followed by a diagnosis and meds, you could have a brighter, more content dog again.

One five-year-old dog I know very well came to see me, and I noticed that she seemed different. She was lacklustre and her hair had thinned, albeit only slightly, and more obviously on her head and her tail. Looking for any other signs, I noticed she had a funny smell about her, too. After a conversation with her loved ones, I learned that she hadn't been herself and had even been weeing on their carpets. I urged them to pay a visit to the vet, who discovered a bad heart murmur, among other things. She is now being treated and on medication and is back to her glorious self. Don't forget dogs are tough blooming cookies. They have a natural instinct to hide pain and weakness, to protect themselves against predators. So it's up to us to become doggy detectives, keeping an eye on them.

There are many different signs to watch out for that may indicate your dog isn't well, including one or more of the following:

- **Lethargy** They will dwell in their beds more than usual and seem to be lacking energy.

- **Reluctance to join in** They don't have the same enthusiasm for their walk or playing at home.

- 🐾 **Decreased appetite** They refuse food, skip meals or just don't regard food with the same interest.

- 🐾 **Excessive licking** Dogs will lick for many positive reasons, including bonding, empathy and love, but also through stress and pain (they will lick sore joints, paws and wounds).

- 🐾 **Increased or decreased urination** You may notice they are going to the toilet more than they would usually – or not at all.

- 🐾 **Increased thirst** Keep an eye on water bowls. Are they getting drained more often than is usual? Do you notice your dog repeatedly visiting the water bowl?

- 🐾 **Excessive panting** Dogs pant to cool themselves down, but also because of stress and pain. So if it isn't hot, why is your dog panting excessively?

- 🐾 **Coughing and sneezing** This could be due to any number of things, including a cold, kennel cough, canine influenza, a respiratory parasite, bacterial/fungal infection, tracheal collapse or even congenital heart failure.

- 🐾 **Shaking** Dogs typically shake when they are cold or nervous, but it can also be a sign of pain.

- 🐾 **Upset bowel movements** Keep an eye on their stools if they are not as firm as usual.

- 🐾 **Dry or itchy skin** Have you noticed your dog scratching themselves a lot? Again, keep an eye on this and check whether they have dandruff or dry skin.

🐾 **Laboured breathing** Any change to their natural breathing pattern when they haven't been exercising would be a warning signal for me.

🐾 **Vomiting** Like us, dogs do throw up, but if your dog is sick more than once, it's always advisable to speak to your vet to make sure it's nothing serious.

🐾 **Unexpected weight loss or gain** You may notice that although you have been feeding and exercising your dog as usual, they are losing or gaining weight.

🐾 **Hair loss** Thinning of hair, especially over their rump (bum) and tail first, could be an early indication of an underlying illness.

🐾 **Pale gums** Gums should be a pink shade, so always keep a check for changes in colour.

🐾 **Bad-temperedness and aggression** When a usually happy and placid dog starts sniping and becoming aggressive, it could be a sign of pain or illness – or even dementia in older dogs.

🐾 **Depression:** be wary of a sad demeanour, not wishing to engage; and likewise check in with their body language – are they hanging their head with their tail down?

🐾 **Change in skin** A dog's skin should bounce back quickly with good elasticity when gently pulled away from their shoulders; if it doesn't, this could be a sign of dehydration.

If you are concerned about any changes in your dog make sure you discuss these with your vet.

4

BEHAVIOUR AND TRAINING

Dog behaviour is a big topic. People tend to think of training a dog in terms of getting them to sit, for example, but rarely do they look deeper into how these complex creatures' minds work. And although we will never completely understand dogs and their ways, the advice I offer here will definitely help you to raise a well-rounded, happy and balanced dog, from the heady days of puppyhood right through to their old age.

A good place to start is with your own mindset, accepting that a dog is still a dog and with that come shredded-up tissues and the occasional drink from a toilet bowl. But dogs don't respond well to shouting, bad moods, irrationality or a lack of enrichment. Taking on a dog is like making a pact to be the best version of yourself with them, and your partnership should be one based on trust and love.

My dogs aren't trained much – they don't know how to roll over; they don't know how to give their paw; nor do they know *not* to chew up the sofa. Confused? Well, I focus instead on ensuring they are mentally strong and balanced, happy and fulfilled. Dogs don't usually want to tear your sofa into a trillion pieces, nor do they wish to poop near where they lie; these behaviours can sometimes be reactions to being unhappy, unsettled and stressed, and are their way of telling you in the loudest way possible, 'I'm not ok.' What's more, berating them for these acts only causes them more stress and distrust. Yes, it might stop the behaviour, but it's not addressing the cause and will scare them into not expressing themselves.

The focus shouldn't be on raising a robotic dog who never steps out of line because they have been forced to behave in a certain way, but on giving them a loving and exciting home life, so their needs are met and they aren't bored or lonely. Once that's achieved, you will notice these unwanted behaviours will go away on their own with little or no training needed.

Also, if your dog is chewing on yet another Disney princess that was left on the carpet, remember that they don't know the difference between what is designed to be chewed and what isn't. So show them. Gently guide them. Swap out contraband with a toy from their own toy box. Dogs love having their own dedicated box – one they can visit to find something to play with on their own or bring to you to instigate a game.

Training a dog is simple if they are fulfilled. But to my mind, it should always be secondary to ensuring their mental needs are met, which is where all the games, walks and other ideas discussed throughout this book come in. You must address every aspect of their health and well-being, through quality nutrition and exercise (both physical and mental), ensuring they are confident and comfortable in their own skin and content when left on their own and that they feel safe and loved. Once all this has been taken care of, you are unlikely to see unwanted behaviours.

So whatever helps you to find your inner zen to become the best trainer for your dog – do it. Whether you get your chill from physical exercise, yoga, meditation, a quick five-minute breathing practice or reading a book, take that time for yourself. Because a happier you means a happier dog.

Positive Reward-Based Training

Thinking of training your dog? There are many methods out there, but the only way to go if you want to maintain that relationship built on trust and mutual respect is positive training.

Put simply, this means we reward the good behaviour and ignore the bad, with bribery (in the form of food, favourite toys or love and attention), kindness and encouragement all the way.

When I have training time with my dog, I use a high-value treat – that high-voltage-wag kind of treat – for maximum engagement. This will be something like liver or freshly cooked chicken – something they really want to work hard for; not their usual kibble, but not a meal either – you only need to reward with the smallest of morsels: titbits. This serves to maintain their focus when you are working on training, so they're not distracted, chomping away on a lump of food. Plus, it keeps a check on their weight – because most dogs love good food as much as we do. If your dog isn't so motivated by food, though, you should use a toy – a special one that's not kept with the others and only comes out at training times. What makes it so special? I hear you ask. Well, you do. You make it super fun for your dog to interact with the toy, playing Fetch or Tug or whatever is their preference.

So you've got the reward, but what do I mean by positive reward-based training? In essence, if you see something you like, you reward it. And you have to be punctual with your rewarding, so get yourself a trendy bum bag, so your reward is in there ready to go.

Speaking for myself, I've never got along with clickers. We have too many things to hold as it is, especially on a walk, what with bagged poop, a lead and keeping one hand free to access the reward, so a clicker, for me, is just another thing to carry. Instead, I use a word to mark the action or behaviour I like. I use 'yes' – just a snappy, calm 'yes' – and then I reward. That way, the dog can easily figure out what it is I liked; it's your own verbal 'click'.

Training is pretty mentally tiring for dogs, so don't expect too much at the beginning. You will lose their concentration if you attempt sessions that are too long or complex. Start small and build up the skill level and duration. Then, as your training progresses, mix things up and increase the difficulty to keep things spicy and interesting.

'You Can't Teach an Old Dog New Tricks'

This is a fib! Yes, they are much more mouldable when they are pups, but you can teach an oldie or mid-lifer a new trick, too. The harder part is getting them to want to work it out, to relearn previous behaviours and start to problem solve again, like they did when they were pups. The greatness that can be achieved when there's a sliver of sausage in the balance is amazing.

The bottom line here is that if you have a dog already, but aren't spending much time keeping their mind active, it isn't too late to start. You can still train them to heel or come back or even close your fridge door (this, in particular, helps enormously with my late-evening snacking).

Consistency and Routine

If you are a creature of habit who sticks to a pattern pretty closely day to day, and your dog is bound by this, they will become familiar with their regime and get used to doing things in a certain way and at particular times. Some dogs find a routine settling and reassuring, but if they rely on it too heavily and you decide to go for an impromptu early meal out one day, it can upset them when they are used to a strict structure.

My mum's dog, for instance, darts off to the kitchen every day at 4.30pm, licking her lips, knowing full well that if she makes her presence known, dinner will very quickly be served. I have no idea how she even knows the time!

I am an early bird, so my dogs are used to getting up and out at 6.30am. If I were to stay upstairs for an extra hour, the dogs would be whinging away downstairs and crossing their little legs, as they'd need their morning tinkle. They are used to my routine. Which means no lie-ins for me (not that I'm permitted them anyway, as my children are my alarm clocks, jumping on my bed in the early hours).

Routine for a dog helps to alleviate anxiety; they don't have to worry about what's happening next, as they already know. Survival and food are of primary importance to them, so taking away the stress of knowing when their next meal is ensures they can just enjoy life and all the small things – the attention, the walks, the stimulation.

When you have a new dog, consistency and routine also help them to settle quickly. They will feel secure and become house trained faster. When feeding and treat times are planned out, it also serves to prevent unnecessary weight gain in your dog because they know, for example, they'll get that bedtime biscuit when they get into their bed at night. (My dogs love their bedtime treat, even if it is a dried chicken heart! And they won't let me forget it either. They are delighted to do a running jump into their beds, knowing night time isn't so bad.)

Set a routine that suits you and the dog. But that means that even the morning after a heavy Friday night out, you'll still have to crawl down those stairs to see your pal, regardless of how rough you feel. That is all part of the commitment you make when taking on a dog.

Being Present

Life is a rat race and as we are all hustling to make a living, it's easy to forget to be present, to be calm and to live in the moment. As we become more and more fast-paced, we also become more stressed and anxious, and this can easily transfer on to our dogs. There are many simple ways to learn to be more at peace in our minds. Understanding what a positive impact this has will be such a game changer for you, especially in terms of your energy, which feeds your fuzz head.

Living in the here and now, being present, is a great tool to help us navigate the world we live in. Dogs, like us, don't always live in the present. They too worry; they may worry about that dog they came across in the park last week or those crazy big buses that whoosh past them when they leave the house with Mama and turn left on to the high street. We see this a lot in rescue dogs, where previous experience and environment affect their thinking and behaviour (just as it can for us). Even more reason why we need to become the zen masters of dog guardianship (more on this in the next chapter)!

Here are some great tips to help you build a better connection with your dog:

🐾 Enjoy walks without your phone. It's all too easy to pavement pound while scrolling away, but taking that time to enjoy the walk, connect with your dog and appreciate the great outdoors together is mutually beneficial.

🐾 Take time with training (see p. 73).

Mindful tip

Exercise is such a large proportion of what we do with our dogs. And mindfulness can happen at any time, even when you are moving around; it doesn't have to be all about yoga mats and sitting still.

Often, when we prepare for a run or a walk, it's all automated – we put on our shoes and pick up that lead on autopilot. Instead, try mixing up your routine and thinking about where you are going to go, what you will see and why you are doing it. Is it to live longer? Be healthier? Be more energetic? Spend time with your dog?

Do you usually reach for the headphones and listen to your favourite playlist? Leave them at home and instead be fully present and enjoy the world around you, soaking up your surroundings. What can you hear? What is the weather like? Can you guess the temperature? Notice the footpath you are walking along.

Pay close attention to your body, too: feel your feet striking the ground again and again, feel the muscles in your legs working and your arms moving from side to side. Notice your breathing – breathe deeper, observing the pattern and repetition.

It's ok for your mind to wander – that's natural – but once you realise that's happened, let those thoughts float away and bring yourself back into the present.

Finally, take time to stop, check in with your partner in crime and smile. Remember, even on days when you don't feel so happy, forcing a smile can lift your spirits.

- When you give them their lovely big snugs, check in with them – make sure they are well and content, using your inner telepathy skills and looking for signs (see p. 47). You will get to know your dog's different moods pretty quickly.

- Put your phone in a drawer for a few hours every evening to avoid checking it all the time, and getting drawn into people's content.

- Try not to engage with the what-if's that can cloud your thoughts. Instead, accept that you do have an inner dialogue, but try simply acknowledging those nagging thoughts, thanking them and putting them aside. You can't appreciate the beautiful moments in your life if your mind is filled with negative thoughts and worries.

- Think positive thoughts, enjoying the present moment. It takes practice to reprogramme your thought processes, but it can be done.

Common Issues

The most common problems I tend to see are separation anxiety, pulling on a lead, running off and barking. If you are struggling with any of these but feel that all your dog's needs are being met, it's worth seeking out professional help to try to rectify the problem.

Trainers and behaviourists do different things. A trainer can help with lead-pulling issues and poor recall, for example, but it's a behaviourist who should be looking at things like separation anxiety and aggression, as they have typically trained for longer and have much more in-depth knowledge of a dog's mind.

Training

Finding a good trainer can be tricky. There are so many training methods and ideas as to the 'correct' way to train your dog, so making the right decision is vital to ensure no damage is done. Always look for a positive trainer – one who rewards good behaviour, ignores unwanted behaviour, never uses force and doesn't take anything away. Whether you have a German Shepherd or a Pomeranian, the same approach to their training can be adopted.

Teaching to heel

All too often, I've seen prong collars (metal, with blunt spikes on the inside against the dog's neck) used to stop pulling on large breeds, the idea being that the dog associates the pulling with pain, and they stop pulling because it's painful. (This doesn't stop the dog's urge to pull; it just prevents them from being able to.) This type of training undoes all the work you have done on building trust, with the dog ending up stressed and frustrated. Instead, work on the 'look-at-me' command, bringing the dog's focus back to you, and then reward. Once they are focused on you and realise they got rewarded for it, you can add a marker word like 'heel' and, when they are in the heel position, they get rewarded with a treat and praise. With repetition, you can increase the duration of the heeling to get a reward, and so they learn that it is much nicer to walk near their guardian because cheese rains from the sky and they are showered in praise. With this type of training, the heel becomes a default behaviour.

When you are in the training phase of learning to heel, it's best to use a different lead set and remember to keep your bum bag on you for your clicker, if you use one, and treats;

this way, they will know the difference between when they are working and their down time, when they may still pull. Because your dog still needs a walk in the meantime, and training to heel takes much longer than one or two walks, let them know when it's down time by extending their lead and not using the training lead or the treat-filled bum bag.

Recall

This can be a big problem for some dogs – what's happening on the other side of a field is often far more exciting than what you are doing, after all, especially if you have a lead in hand and they know you want to head home. Dogs do need their freedom to romp about, but they need to be safe, too. So I work on recall when they are very young, but I start it in quieter places first – like inside the house, with not much distance between them and me. (You want to see that excited leap into action when you call them over and reward them with bundles of praise and their toy of the moment or a treat.) Then, incrementally, you build on this, practising recall in the garden or on a quiet walk, using a long line and building on the distraction level and the distance. It's important to reward generously, so don't just take their kibble out – you need a really strong positive association, something top notch on the dog's yummy scale. When your dog returns to you, allow them to move away from you again and return to any sniffing or running around they were previously doing. Otherwise, if every time you call them it results in you working them for a sit and putting their lead on, the association will become a negative one (they're not daft). By mixing it up on walks, it's a gamble for the dog – often it's treats and praise, and sometimes it does mean you are going home, but they are happy to play that recall roulette, as long as you keep it fun.

TEACH YOUR DOG TO 'SPEAK'

I taught my Dobermann to 'speak' and to be quiet. This is pretty easy to do.

Have some delicious cooked chicken at the ready and start doing training. Holding the chicken, encourage them to bark. Dogs are excellent problem solvers, so they will work through their back catalogue of sits, lying down and maybe even a paw, until they realise what you are asking them to do. You don't want them to feel too frustrated about not having the chicken, so as soon as they start making a little noise, you need to reward that, repeating this as they realise that this is what you want, and encouraging them to get louder. Deliver high praise and lots of chicken when that bark comes out. Then, once they have got the gist of what you are training them to do, add in the word 'speak' and reward. Repeat, until they really understand what you are asking. From here, you can train them to be quiet. You have their focus, because you always train with a high-value currency for them, so, when they are barking away, wait for that second when they take a breath – that moment when they just stop for a quick listen – and jump in and reward. Then ask them to sit and look at you and really praise them, as they are no longer barking and are doing just as you are asking. Then ask them to 'speak' again and reward, and, the moment they stop, use a cue word like 'quiet' and reward again immediately. With repeated training to speak and to be quiet, you can use this as a great party trick or to help in those moments when your dog is barking but you want them to stop (see also p. 88–91).

Jumping up

Some breeds are predisposed to be bouncier than others. A Whippet's build, for instance, makes jumping up easy and, coupled with their energetic nature, they can be super bouncy. A Bulldog doesn't have the same energy levels and their build – with fairly short legs and a wide front – means jumping up isn't so comfortable for them. (Having said that, I do know of one bouncy Bulldog who could almost take you out, he is such a strong boy.)

I have some seriously bouncy dogs at home, and I don't mind a bit of jumping up (I like my dogs to be dogs), although it can be a problem when they jump up at strangers, children or passers-by. But, rightly or wrongly, I excuse jumping up with my smaller dogs (all under 7kg) because a two-legged stance is a way for them to get closer to greet or smell us and to get to our faces for a snuffle if we are leaning over. My 4kg girlie has to stand on her back legs for attention, otherwise she would just be engulfed by the bigger dogs. So there are times at home when you are relaxed and can just let them do their thing, but there are also times when they need to keep all four paws on the ground.

If your dog's jumping-up habit is upsetting those around you or becoming a nuisance (especially if they are on the larger side), some training might be needed. And be aware that it's easier to train them not to jump up at you than it is to train them not to jump up at passers-by, visitors or acquaintances out on a walk.

When training, you don't want to restrain them or prevent them from being able to jump up, nor should you inflict pain by lifting up your leg, so that when they jump, they land on your bony knee. These techniques are very old hat, using negative reinforcement. For a happy and trusting relationship you should, again, use positive reinforcement of the behaviour you want to see. This method does take longer, but it's the right way to go.

I once pretended with my Dobermann (rest in peace, Angel) that she'd hurt me jumping up. She was young, but she was big and it was uncomfortable. I'd heard that you could yelp and dogs would really respond to that. So I gave it a whirl and let out an 'Ouch' when she tried to take me out. She immediately changed her energy to calm, giving me an all-knowing look (she was a super-intelligent girl). And she rarely did it again.

The main reason why a dog jumps up is for attention, so the key is removing the attention (i.e. eliminating eye contact, putting your hands away or turning away) and, if they continue, stepping away from them completely. Then, you capture the moment when they stop and look at you and reward that, so they realise that jumping up achieves the exact opposite of what they want (because they get ignored), whereas keeping all four paws on the ground gets them both a reward and your attention. It's as simple as that – but it takes time, and trial and error in different scenarios.

If you do make a plan to stop any jumping up, all members of your household have to be on board and you need to have plenty of treats to hand, so that when someone arrives at your door unexpectedly, you can use that moment as a quick training session.

Note: if you come across a jumpy dog when you're out and about, and their guardian tells you they are training their dog not to jump up at people or that they don't want you to allow them to jump up, you must step back and start the interaction on a calmer level. If, however, they are totally relaxed about the frog-in-a-pump greeting (which is the preferred greeting of my Toy Poodle), then crack on and be prepared for paw prints on trousers.

TARGET STICKS

I love a target stick. (Basically, a telescopic pole with a small rubber ball or 'target' at the end.) I find this a really great tool to start mixing up training, and it's particularly great for rainy days, to add some mental stimulation when you can't get out and about.

You start by putting some food on the end of the target stick and asking your dog to touch it with their nose, using a buzz word, like 'touch'. Then you 'click' or use your marker word when they do this and reward, repeating until you have trained the dog to touch the end of the target.

Next, move the target stick to the side of the dog's face, below them, near their rear, and ask for the 'touch'; once they have done this ,reward. Now practise moving the stick a little further away from the dog, so they have to take a step to touch it, reaffirming the training. Make sure you click or use your marker word the moment their nose touches the stick. Now your dog has mastered how to follow the target stick like a lure, you can use it to teach them many other things, like luring them towards the remote control and replacing the word 'touch' with 'remote', to the washing machine and using the word 'washer' or around an obstacle course. And you can teach them the correct position to walk by you when out and about.

Eventually, with lots of practice the technique can be used to get them to do really fun and useful tricks, like shutting the washing machine-door. It's about time they pulled their weight around the house, isn't it!

Fun, fun, fun

Be fun with your training. Don't worry about looking like a dork. Who cares anyway? Your dog will love you so much for showing them your fun, silly and engaging side and, in turn, they will work so much harder for you. Always be positive, consistent and even a little bit goofy at times to get that interaction. Believe me, at 7am in a windy field on a cold Sunday morning, I really have to work on putting on a good act, but before long I'm actually enjoying myself, too.

Positive training is a lovely way to bond and spend time with your dog, it encourages them to think for themselves and builds confidence. Not only will you have a content dog, but they will learn to trust you so much and you will definitely have fun along the way. You may even get competitive with it and look into obedience trials or start an Instagram page for your dog showcasing their abilities and how you trained them. So many possibilities! Turning your new-found talent as a trainer into a hobby with your dog is a beautiful thing.

Working With a Behaviourist

Some of the issues we have with our dogs' behaviour can be beyond the realms of what we can manage ourselves. Enter the professional behaviourist.

A behaviourist deals with more complex training and behavioural problems in dogs, including aggression, destructive behaviour, obsessions, anxiety and fear, teaching them a different way of life and thinking. Think of a behaviourist as a dog's very own psychologist, with an in-depth knowledge of how their mind works and why they think or feel a certain way.

Separation anxiety

Separation anxiety is a complicated and much-discussed issue for many pet parents. And it seems to be on the rise post pandemic, as a lot of young dogs were used to having the family around them all the time and then, all of a sudden, they are left alone. It's a big adjustment for them and some don't settle too well.

So what are the signs that your dog is suffering from separation anxiety?

Well, there are the more obvious ones, like excessive barking when they are left, defecating, scratching at doorways and even ignoring their stuffed food toy because they are too upset. Or they can be unsettled, panting and looking worried, becoming more het up when they notice your departing cues (like getting keys, putting on shoes and a coat). Then, when you return home, they'll be over the top with their greeting, desperately hoping you will never abandon them to visit the corner shop again. (These are the pooches that typically love to follow you around, watch you on the toilet and whine when you are out of sight.) It's also worth knowing that separation anxiety could be an issue with your dog without you even noticing it; not all dogs will be barking and scratching, destroying things and upsetting the neighbours – some suffer in silence, retreating to their beds, shivering, hiding or pacing around.

Nowadays, you can pick up a web camera inexpensively, so if you need some peace of mind when you are out, this allows you to keep an eye on their behaviour and start to notice cues that they are lonely and anxious, as often these are more apparent when we aren't there to witness them. Treating the problem depends on the severity of the behaviour, but a qualified behaviourist is definitely the way to go when trying to help your dog recover.

You also need to take steps at home to ensure your dog

has a comfortable bed area and knows this is where they can safely relax. It's essential that they get plenty of quality walks and stimulation, so their mind and body are tired and more inclined to just chill out. Insufficient fulfilment, stimulation, enrichment and exercise are big contributors to separation anxiety.

The other thing you can do is to go right back to the beginning of your leaving-the-house routine and watch your dog's body language. Try to identify the point at which you think they've realised you are about to go out and intercept that moment, so that you can recondition your dog to look forward to you putting your shoes on and popping out because, boy oh boy, they are going to get something they really want. Practising your leaving routine (only without actually leaving), building up in small steps and rewarding your dog throughout is a good start to helping them feel less anxious when you do go out. And patience is a must. All this in conjunction with consulting a professional can really help you to put a good plan in place for your dog's recovery.

Aggression

Aggression in dogs is a serious problem, but there are multiple ways of approaching the issue, depending on the trigger. Here again, getting a dog behaviourist involved is essential. And the sooner the better, as aggression – whether towards people, other dogs or other animals – can quickly escalate.

Any dog is capable of being aggressive. It's not a breed-specific problem and even the most beautifully tempered dog can snap if they are constantly bothered and just want to be left alone, or if they are pushed into a corner, by another dog, say, and feel threatened.

Dogs have an innate fight-or-flight mechanism, and

sometimes they feel the need to 'fight' – but this can soon become a learned behaviour. For instance, if they are nervous around other dogs and one runs up to them in the park when they're on the lead and they can't run away (flight), they resort to their default (fight).

Aggression (in any form) is one of the main reasons why dogs are turned in to rescue centres, and, because it's hard for staff there to work on their issues when they're not in a 'normal' environment, these dogs end up being overlooked and, sadly, some are euthanised. So don't put aggression on the back burner to sort next week. It's your duty to get a handle on it as soon as possible to ensure that both you and your dog, as well as the general public, other animals, people you live with and any visitors to your home are safe.

There are many different types of aggression in dogs – fear aggression, protective aggression, pain-induced aggression, defensive aggression, frustrated aggression, redirected aggression, territorial aggression, possessive aggression, social aggression, predatory aggression and sex-related aggression – so dealing with it is not a one-size-fits-all scenario. A behaviourist will observe your dog's behaviour to understand what the problem is, and then formulate a plan of action accordingly.

Muzzle training is important for any dog showing signs of aggression, so they need to accept the muzzle and associate it with something positive – for example, when the muzzle comes out, so does the fresh chicken. A muzzle is for everyone's safety while training is in progress. They are also super handy for vet visits if your dog isn't a fan of going there.

If aggression suddenly arises in a previously non-aggressive dog or increases in a previously somewhat aggressive dog, it's worth taking them to the vet to ensure they are not in pain or experiencing an underlying problem that may be creating or exacerbating the behaviour. (When dogs are in pain, poorly or going senile they can suddenly become aggressive.)

Dog Etiquette

Dog etiquette differs from training in that it is more about teaching socially acceptable behaviour – a bit like going to doggy finishing school. Broadly speaking, it's often more for the benefit of those around you than for you – but it will benefit you, too.

Teaching your dog manners is important. Take barking, for example – while it is, of course, a normal expression of being a dog, it is poor etiquette for a dog to bark at everyone who walks into the café you're sitting in.

Training your dog in social etiquette means you will be more relaxed, knowing they are just being a total poppet and they are relaxed because they know their boundaries and can enjoy fun days out with the family, trips to the coffee shop for a biscuit and an ear tickle or a Saturday-evening early-doors drink with the possibility of a Mini Cheddar in the local.

Etiquette around food

In the same way that I tell my children not to talk with their mouths open and blow their noses constantly during cold season, my dogs have to conform, too.

Is this natural for them? Well, no. They just want to jump all over us, play 'the floor is lava' on our furniture and kitchen surf the worktops for sandwiches. But this doesn't make for great cohabiting. So going back to those boundaries we talked about earlier, we need to think more about what we think is acceptable and unacceptable behaviour and let our dogs know what we are happy with. Of course, we must accept that dogs will be dogs and there will be mishaps and bin raids, but we should be working on etiquette continuously, so that we have a well-rounded dog we can take to friends' houses for barbecues, without fearing that they will snatch a sausage out of someone's hand. Teaching them 'manners' will make life with them a little less hectic, giving you peace of mind, safe in the knowledge that you can take them pretty much anywhere or into any situation and they won't show themselves – or you – up.

The most common food etiquette issues I've come across are jumping on worktops or at people, snatching food and begging at the table (the little piggies do like their food).

When it comes to our family mealtimes, I don't want the dogs all begging at the table and, as I have small children who drop food and small dogs that circle the table like piranhas in a horror movie, I ask them to sit in their beds. I don't feed them from the table and, although I do allow them to have leftovers, it's always in their bowl at their mealtimes.

If I have a houseful and food is out, then I put the dogs away in the utility room, as I just can't keep my eye on them all the time. I know of one dog that pinched a chicken satay – complete with the skewer – from a garden party and have heard more times than I can count about dogs pinching chocolate at Christmas, ending in emergency vet visits. You have to be so careful. If you choose to give your dog non-dog foods, you need to know which are unsafe (see box, p. 86). Or you may decide upon zero human food, and that's ok, too.

So how do we go about addressing those 'quirks' in dogs' behaviour around food in a kind and thoughtful way?

For kitchen side surfers, first make life easier for yourself by putting all food away. A roast chicken left steaming on the side while you pop to answer the door is so tempting for a dog with a super-powered nose. In that scenario, try to get into the habit of taking the dog with you to the hallway, letting it pop outside for a cruise around the garden or putting the chicken back in the oven.

That aside, of course it's not hygienic to have their paws all over the place so, for side surfers, you have to catch them in the act – dogs simply don't understand what you are talking about if you try to train retrospectively. You need to teach them the 'Off' or 'Down' command (you choose your word) and use this training to get them down, off your furniture, off you and off the dining-room table. Dogs are opportunist scavengers, after all.

You have to show them what you mean with the 'down' command, so I use the vocal cue 'Down' or 'Off', have a high-value treat at the ready (remember, we always have to make the training positive) and guide them down, using the treat as a lure. When all four feet are on the floor, I say 'Yes' and reward. Consistency is key, and they will soon understand that this command means 'All four feet on the floor, please.'

A good training trick to help your dogs with food snatching and when you are cooking and accidentally drop something is to teach them to 'leave it'. Start with a treat in your fist, and allow the dog to sniff it. They may start to nuzzle your fist, trying to open your hand for the tasty morsel, but you should keep it closed, using the words 'leave it', and, in the split second when the dog stands back and stops sniffing your hand, or looks up at you like 'What's all this about, Mum?' then immediately reward. Repeat, using the cue 'leave it', until that gap gets longer and longer and reward. You can make it more complicated by taking a step back, then popping the treat on the floor (don't let them dive in and get it, though, as this will set you way back). They will soon understand the command. Repetition is important. Set two minutes aside each day to reinforce this. Training really gets their brains working and, when done correctly, is a great bonding exercise, too.

UNSAFE FOODS FOR DOGS

🐾 **Raisins, currants and sultanas** These are some-times hidden in cakes and biscuits or scattered around your home by a toddler! They contain a toxin that can cause liver damage and kidney failure in dogs.

🐾 **Cooked bones** Dogs love to chew, but cooked bones can easily splinter and cause damage to their insides. If consumed for too long, they can also cause constipation.

🐾 **Chocolate** Especially around Christmas and Easter, chocolate is sometimes left all over your home. It contains an ingredient called theobro-mine (dark chocolate has the highest content), which is poisonous to dogs and can cause serious kidney failure.

🐾 **Grapes** Like raisins, they contain a toxin that could cause kidney failure or liver damage; they could also be a choking hazard for some dogs.

🐾 **Onions, garlic and chives** These may be hidden in the food we innocently give our dogs as left-overs in their dinner – the gravy from your roast or the stuffing from your Sunday dinner, for example. Whether cooked or raw, the onion family is toxic to dogs and can cause intestinal irritation and red-blood-cell damage. Sometimes the effects of onion consumption (such as lethargy, pale gums, reddish urine, fainting or decreased appetite) aren't seen until several days later.

🐾 **Corn on the cob**: I had first-hand experience of the damage a corn husk can do when my Dobermann raided my mum's compost heap unbeknown to us and nearly lost her life (more of which on p. 134). Corn husks can't be digested, so if consumed, they will basically plug dogs' intestines and cause a blockage.

🐾 **Macadamia nuts** These contain a toxin that affects dogs' nervous system. Be aware that macadamia nuts can be found in pie crusts, cookies and desserts.

🐾 **Avocados** These contain persin, which can cause vomiting and diarrhoea in dogs.

🐾 **Alcohol** Alcohol can be dangerous, even in the smallest quantities. It can cause damage to the central nervous system, as well as sickness and diarrhoea.

🐾 **Caffeine** As with alcohol, dogs are highly sensitive to the effects of caffeine-containing drinks. Even a few sips could lead to sickness, while a higher consumption of caffeine could lead to poisoning.

🐾 **Artificial sweetener** Xylitol can be found in so many of the sweet treats we consume – even some of the peanut butters you may think about

Barking

Barking is an important part of dog communication, but excessive barking can be unneighbourly and, well, a bit annoying. Especially if, like me, you have multiple dogs and one is more reactive to noise, it can set off all the others and then pandemonium ensues.

Never tell your dog off for barking, as this will only make them anxious and confused. After all, think about what you sound like to a dog when you raise your voice – they can't understand what you're saying, so you simply come across as if you are joining in the chorus.

Instead, try to find out what their triggers are. Are they overly anxious? If so, they could be barking out of fear. Could they be trying to protect you and their space a little too zealously? Or maybe they are bored and unstimulated and are barking as a way of letting off steam? To help these problems, you need to try to find a cure for the underlying issues.

For example, if they are barking out of boredom, you'll need to introduce more mental stimulation and exercise into their lives to tire their mind. If they are barking because they are anxious, establish what it is they are anxious about and work on their confidence around that through positive association. And if they are overzealous in guarding you and/or the property, I would focus on why this is – often, a dog is territorial because their needs aren't being fulfilled, or they are not in a calm state and settled in their environment. Try using an anxiety wrap (see p. 169) to help them feel more secure, enrich their minds with puzzle toys and keep them busy with long-lasting treats.

I ignore barking for the most part. Ignoring unwanted behaviour is really important, so I turn away, ensure no eye contact at all, then, when they stop (they always take a moment in their barking cycle), that's when I jump in and reward.

I think that barking at people approaching our homes has increased since the pandemic, when there were no visitors and the only people approaching our doors were making deliveries. And you can see how this might look from the dog's point of view: the doorbell rings, they bark like mad, you open the door, a delivery person passes over a parcel and then disappears. To a dog, this equals intruder alert. They think, I'll warn everyone – and then, when said 'intruder' leaves, the dog thinks, Oh look, it worked! Must do that again next time.

So training is important here. If my doorbell has rung and all the dogs bark, that's totally acceptable; but if I have acknowledged the door and they are still going on and on, I will turn and block them from racing to the door. Then I will wait until there is quiet before scattering tiny morsels of their treats over the floor to distract them, so that they are no longer barking and instead, they have something fun to do. It's an idea to start training your dogs by asking some-one in the household to knock on your door (or, if you are a fast mover, you can do it yourself and then quickly whizz inside before the dogs reach the door).

If your dog barks at people or other dogs when they are

out of the home, you can use food rewards as a distraction. That way, instead of barking, they are focused on you and something good is happening. Whenever they take a breath from barking and look away, that's when you need to reward; as ever, be on the money with that timing – it's always key. It takes a while, but every time you see a dog or pass someone, keep their focus on you as much as possible and, when they start to get excited, bring their focus back to you. In that moment when they stop leaping and look at your face, give a verbal cue (like a calm 'Yes') and feed. Reward them with something uber tasty (not their regular kibble, which they have morning and night, but something really alluring and delicious, like cooked liver). Soon, they will be looking at you more and more and not so interested in the passers-by. This also helps to socialise them, giving them time to safely play and interact with other people and dogs.

Excessive-barking training takes time and patience, but your ears will thank you for your efforts – as will your neighbours and your dog, too.

We can always see behaviours in our dogs that need remedying and where more training is needed, but don't forget to reward them when they are being good and when they are being quiet. I'd use the word 'settle' when they are around the house and being really good and calm but also pacing or standing around and you want them to go and lie somewhere quietly. Invite them or lure them to their bed or the rug where they like to be and then ask them to lie down. Sit beside them and, once you feel them relax, reward very calmly. Then repeat this, until they know what you are asking them to do, then add in the word 'settle' and reward. Practise this daily – and it's super handy to have a pot of small titbits in the fridge door, so you can just do small bursts of training between other activities, like cooking your dinner. If they then naturally go to settle in their favourite spot, go over and tell them how good they are being. It's easy to overlook this good behaviour and focus only on the bouncing, barking fuzz ball demanding your attention, but those moments of quiet calm should be recognised, too.

Barging
All dogs can be bargers (I'm not even sure if that's a word, but you know what I mean – when they push past you through doorways, barge into other dogs on walks and block and shove you around the house when you are not moving or where they want you to be). You may have a small dog, so that their barging mostly goes unnoticed, or a large one who runs over your feet and legs, leaving you hopping in pain. I have owned a particularly bargy dog. He was enormous – we are talking small-Great-Dane size – and I swear, when I first got him (he was a rescue), he aimed for the backs of my knees, knowing full well this was a weak spot. He even sent me to the doctor's when, travelling at about 30mph, he barrel-rolled me across a field! It was a big, open space and he just ran at me full speed and took me out. Apparently, I did a full flip – and believe me, I'm no gymnast, so it was a first for me. This cheeky chap also used to barge other dogs on walks, often using the barrel-rolling technique on them, too, literally throwing his weight around. I knew it was something I had to address before someone else or another dog got hurt. I also couldn't understand why he was doing it, so I had to figure this out. (I thought it might have been purely down to bad manners, as he had grown up in a kennel before coming to me and just acted on impulse without thinking about anything else.) Dogs will barge into you and other dogs for many reasons: because they are impatient or they haven't learned their 'manners'; or it could be attention-seeking behaviour or because they want something from you. But it isn't because they are being 'dominant' or 'wanting to be top dog' – that old theory has been discredited.

Whatever the cause, because we are in a leadership role, we need to guide them in learning the behaviours we want to see. I managed to rectify the pushing-about issue with my rescue dog through general obedience and manners training, as well as lots of fulfilment (allowing him to be a dog, sniffing, walking, snoozing and letting him love and be loved). He became much less excitable and het up all the time. And I learned to read when he was getting carried away and his arousal levels were too high (overstimulated). With settling-in time – into our home and routines and within the pack of dogs – he stopped feeling the need to mow things down and became a relaxed, calmer, happier dog.

If you are having an issue with this, it can mean that off-the-lead walking is stopped until the problem is resolved. And there are loads of brilliant dog trainers out there who can help with this.

Avoiding Instilling Inappropriate Behaviours

I think I've already made it clear here, and it is also widely understood that a positive, reward-based training regime is best for our dogs. Nevertheless, there are things we do, sometimes every day and often without knowing, that set in habits in our dogs, whether we intend to or not. And we all do it.

Take this, for example: you come home, having been out at the shops, and make a great fuss of your dog – so much so that anyone would think you had returned after a year backpacking around Australia. For a dog that doesn't mind its own company, this would be fine. But for one that feels more anxious when you leave the house, if only to buy some bread and milk, it can soon become an emotional trigger for them, and something that gets worse, becoming a 'thing' – an unwanted behaviour. Honestly, I've seen this more times than I have had hot dinners and it can start young.

Puppies are mollycoddled (rightly so, to some extent, because they are just too delicious). They are carried around, never left and, when they are upset – even for a second – you come back to them. To the extent that when you return after having just been in another room, they leap around like uncoordinated frogs because they are just so delighted to see you.

The mistake then is that you fuss too much and make a big song and dance about seeing them again, scooping them up, caressing them, telling them you missed them so much . . . And the dog thinks, Yeah, oh gosh, it was so tough, wasn't it? Let' s never ever – pinkie promise – ever be apart again. This is a prime example of how we set in behaviours in anxious dogs; how repeatedly reacting with an over-the-top response can reaffirm clinginess, leading them to think it is a wanted behaviour, which can then escalate.

I always offer my dogs attention, love and understanding but, when they are being super clingy, it's all about keeping things calm and not inducing a state of anxiety. It's absolutely ok to reassure a worried dog, but your energy and timing have to be right and an excessive greeting can escalate into sheer panic in the dog at being apart from you, however briefly, if repeated over a period of time. It's much better to return home in a relaxed way and to greet your dog when they are chill about the situation as well.

We've already looked at jumping up and barking, but what about other common unwanted behaviours that are all too easily set in – things like mouthing, begging and looking for mischief?

Mouthing

Opinion is divided on this one. Some people think it's unacceptable and some don't mind it, as long as it's gentle. It can be viewed as a natural expression, a normal primeval instinct as they can feel so much through their mouths.

Some dogs mouth much more than others. I have dogs who poke me – yes, literally poke me – with their noses in the backs of my legs for attention; and my Dobie used to tuck her head in between my legs, so I could 'diddle' her ears when she was excited (she often did this with strangers, too, which was rather disconcerting for them). They all have their own little personalities and idiosyncrasies that make them as unique and individual as we are. But I have one dog in particular who loves to mouth. It's simply her greeting. She never ever bites, but when she's excited she will mouth my hand (she's only 4kg, so it's a bit like a piglet suckling) and, rightly or wrongly, it's just so cute and hilarious because she's so sweet with it.

Seeing my dogs show happiness makes me happy, too, and mouthing is generally done in excitement, for attention and for play. It is rarely a sign of aggression, but it can escalate or be too full on, so it does need to be monitored.

If your dog's mouthing is too hard or they get too carried away, it's a good idea to train them out of it. Training with mouthing should be done gently and calmly and not turned into a tug-me-pull-me game. As always, ignore unwanted behaviour and reward the good. Encourage them to get a toy and bring that to you instead – that way they have fun interacting with their toys.

Begging

Begging can easily become habitual, especially when a high-value food is involved – that delicious corner of a Yorkshire pudding or a sneaky, crispy roast potato being handed down from the table. And it can often go unnoticed, especially if you have an eight-year-old version of me at your table who is sick at the thought of salmon on a Thursday night!

It's entirely up to you how you wish your dog to behave around food. Feeding them from the table might be completely acceptable to you, but confusion can arise when your great-aunt comes round for Sunday lunch and chastises them for begging. So set your table rules and stick to them, so that everyone – including (or especially) your dog – knows what is and isn't ok.

Looking for mischief

Bored dogs will look for mischief, but you don't want the pleasure they find in gnawing at that chair leg to become their go-to comforter when they are alone. Instead, think about the why behind the behaviour: why aren't they fulfilled and settled enough during the day to be content just relaxing and sleeping? If they are young, are they teething? Do they need a chew? Are they stressed when you leave? Try to work out what's causing the behaviour, so that you can address it before it becomes embedded. For the most part, a contented, fulfilled, exercised dog won't get up to serious mischief in your home.

I think the biggest takeaway for you here is that, although none of us will have the perfect dog, many behavioural issues can be ironed out with the right physical and mental stimulation – playing games, interaction, cuddle time and allowing them the freedom to sniff and explore. The fulfilment that all these things bring leaves little room for excess energy or unwanted behaviours.

5

THE ZEN MASTER OF DOG GUARDIANS

Ok, this is the goal – my aim as my dog's custodian: I want to be the zen master of dog guardians. I want to be that calm, chill, understanding and reliable dog mama who offers a loving, comfortable and balanced environment for their dog to live in.

Well, like I said, that is the goal. But in reality, it's something I have to work on every day. My home is chaos. I have four dogs, two very small children. My house has been undergoing a full renovation, and the dust – I can't tell you how I battle with dust. Not to mention juggling my work and various side hustles.

So am I that perfect person? No, I'm not. I know my limitations. And I know when it's all just a bit much – when I'm tired, when the puppy has de-stuffed a dog bed or chewed up my son's favourite *Paw Patrol* character. I can see my emoji icon as that dude with steam coming out of his ears. But, importantly, I do recognise when I'm feeling stretched. Then I'll talk to my husband and take ten minutes to sit and meditate (I'm learning and getting better at this) and then list my tasks with a priority scale. And I know these things make me feel better.

Inside, I may be thinking, Aaaaaaaaargh, when I come downstairs to find a dog on my dining table and a shredded house plant, but I try not to let it show, remaining calm, swapping out any contraband and replacing it with something they are allowed. Then I ask myself why this has happened – why are they so bored that they are getting themselves into mischief?

The following are signs that your dog may be bored:

🐾 Chewing

🐾 Escaping the garden

🐾 Digging

🐾 Pacing

🐾 Panting without reason

🐾 Running away

🐾 Overexcitement

🐾 Scratching

🐾 Excessive licking

And some possible reasons:

🐾 They have missed a walk.

🐾 They've had insufficient exercise or stimulation.

🐾 They are home alone a lot.

🐾 They don't have a proper schedule or routine.

🐾 They're lacking socialisation.

🐾 They need more toys to play with or chews of their own.

You should not yell or lose control ever. And telling them 'No' after the event doesn't have any effect either – if you don't catch your dog in the act, you'll be wasting your breath and energy. Instead, let it go, count to five in your head, take deep breaths and tidy the bomb site. It's amazing how different you'll feel taking those few seconds to breathe and count, rather than letting yourself feel cross, which serves no purpose and will only make you feel bad afterwards.

To be the zen master of dogs, we should lead by example and keep a lid on things, no matter the situation. But we are all human and must first accept that we are not perfect (maybe nearly, but not quite!). So it's about learning, recognising yourself and continually improving. Because, ultimately – in my case, at least – I want to do the best by my children and my animals. And that's why I strive to be that zen master.

Remember also not to hold a grudge. Just let those feelings go and accept that dogs will be dogs.

Here are some practical tips to set you on the path to zen masterhood:

🐾 Change your environment – go into another room or outside.

🐾 If you have a dog who de-stuffs, get stuffing-free toys and use a plastic or wicker bed with fleecy vet-type bedding or blankets in the bottom.

🐾 Get plant stands for your house plants. (I have done this and so eliminated the possibility of my small dogs tipping over the plants; granted, they'll now pull out the loo paper in the downstairs toilet and shred it instead, but as long as we remember to keep the door shut, that doesn't happen either).

And some tips to help you internally when you're trying to be zen:

- **Breathing** Spend as little as one minute taking slow and deep breaths, concentrating on your breaths in and out.

- **Recalibrate your brain** When a negative thought comes in, accept it, then let it go and swap in a positive one. So if you are thinking, I've got too much work on today, follow it up with something like this: But aren't I so lucky to be busy; how blessed am I?

- **Music** Your choice of music not only affects your mood but your dog's as well. I have a playlist I like to start the day with; it's full of toe-tapping, joyous songs that set me up right. Try this, if you are feeling stressed. It's amazing how the rise and fall of a beautiful classical piece, for example, will reset your mood.

- **Talk (or write) it out** It feels good to share a problem with someone understanding, even if there is no solution. And if you don't have someone to discuss it with right at that time, try writing it down. It's amazing how much better you feel when it's out of your head.

- **Sleep** We all know how important sleep is, so turn off the box, put your phone away, read a book after a relaxing bath (oh my days, with clean sheets, too – heavenly). That's a happy place right there. Plus, we are so different when we have had plenty of sleep. I know I am a better version of myself when I am well slept. If

I have had a rough night's sleep or been up and down with the children, I can feel myself being much more short-tempered.

And several things you can do in your direct dealings with your dog:

🐾 **Food** Feed your dog the best food for optimal nutrition, ensuring that you exclude E-numbers and sugars from their diet (see Chapter 7 for more on this).

🐾 **Stimulation** Create a stimulating life for your dog with plenty of variety (new places for walks, new patches to sniff and christen), allowing them to just be a dog (doing doggy things, meeting other dogs) and having plenty of interaction, engaging with them, playing games and training.

🐾 **Education** Educate yourself by reading and understanding your dog more (you have made the right start by reading this book – we have established you are a caring dog guardian).

🐾 **Understanding** Demonstrate lots of understanding towards your dog and their behaviour, gently showing them their boundaries, so they can enjoy some structure in their life.

🐾 **Be calm** Being a calm and balanced guardian will benefit you, your dog and everyone around you.

Know that you are both in it for the long haul, warts and all, and by caring about their health and wellbeing, you will be caring about your own health and wellbeing, too – making you the zen master of dogs.

Mindful Practices

Mindfulness is much talked about, and I have already touched on mindful practices in this book. But why is it so important – especially in relation to having a dog?

Mindfulness is a type of meditation or way of thinking that focuses the mind, so you are paying attention to something, slowing down and taking your time in a relaxed way. It can be used during meditation, but also in everyday tasks, like breathing exercises or when you are doing your regular dog walk. Mindfulness may sound a bit woo woo, but it helps to alleviate everyday stresses and anxiety and helps us to regulate our own emotions. It also helps us to be less distracted by things around us, as well as improving our sleep.

Mindfulness can be looked at as an essential skill that we all need; perhaps that's why it's even being introduced to young children in schools in England – because it really is such a valuable tool for dealing with life.

Mindfulness can be broken down broadly into several categories, including:

🐾 mindful breathing

🐾 mindful observation

🐾 mindful appreciation

🐾 mindful awareness.

Mindful breathing

This is super simple and really helps to ease stress. It's about focusing only on your breath – in and out, in its natural form – and is a great tool to bring you back into balance when you start to feel emotional or stressed. I set out a bed on my living-room floor for my dog and sit on the floor myself to practise breathing. Similarly, so long as your dog is a willing participant, get them settled with you and have that connection with them; you may be giving them a gentle tickle or simply laying your hands on them. Then close your eyes and breathe, sense yourself relaxing, sense your dog relaxing. Gorgeous. You should notice that afterwards you feel much lighter and calmer.

Mindful observation

Mindful observation is about noticing something – say, a flower, or taking a blanket into the garden with your dog on a clear day or night and looking up at the clouds or the stars and the moon and just basking in the natural beauty. Watch your chosen subject as if you are seeing it for the first time, in awe, in true appreciation of the amazing natural beauty all around you. Don't think about what's for dinner – let that go. Just be present and enjoy the peace and the beauty, letting it envelop you. If you focus on a cloud, say, and nothing else for even a minute, it's amazing the peace of mind and stillness you'll achieve. It's divine. And it's important for dogs to enjoy quiet time, too. A 2022 study published in the *International Journal of Mental Health and Addiction* showed that nature therapy helped as a short-term treatment for many mental-health conditions, including anxiety.[1] It's all around us. And it's free!

---

1 https://link.springer.com/article/10.1007/s12144-022-03421-3

Mindful appreciation

This is about being grateful and giving thanks for the smaller things in life – things we sometimes take for granted. Practising gratitude helps you to be more present and to live mindfully. It can be a way of life, transforming the way you look and feel about everything. I love to practise gratitude and wake every morning thinking about something positive. Naturally, we all have some negative thoughts, whether about the weather or the way we feel, but I try to recognise my negative thoughts and then change them to something positive – how, if it's raining, I won't have to do any watering. Why not try this as well? Someone just had a bout of road rage at you? Instead of getting worked up and cross about it, be grateful you are safe and that you don't have that level of inner anger. If someone bumped into you and didn't apologise, don't get cross. Instead, be grateful that your mama taught you great manners – they cost nothing. We can all take a moment each day to appreciate the people and animals around us, the food in the fridge, the happy greeter who is so excited to see you, that first cup of tea or coffee that's always the best one of the day and

all the things our friends/family/dogs do to make our day a bit better (the loving optimism I am greeted with when I come downstairs to four wagging bottoms, for example).

You can even make a gratitude list over your morning cuppa. Writing things down can really affirm the practice. Try writing in a journal five things you are most grateful for on any given day. Practising gratitude regularly in this way can re-map the way your brain thinks about things, so that it becomes second nature. And with a guardian who has such a positive outlook and aura, your dog will benefit, too – as will all those around you.

Mindful awareness

Mindful awareness is all about focusing on the emotional state that may arise when being mindful – thinking about how you feel in that moment. Are you feeling happy, optimistic, stressed, anxious? Once you are aware of your emotional state, you can work on why you are feeling that way.

You can also use mindful awareness with your dog, taking time to think about how *they* may be feeling. If you are on a walk, sit together for a moment, look into their eyes and read their body language – are they having a great day? If you are at home, sipping your coffee, observe your dog using mindful awareness: are they restless? Are they relaxed and content? Knowing how your dog is feeling helps you to work on improving their life and mental wellbeing.

Applying mindfulness with your dog

There are many things you do every day with your dog that could benefit from a sprinkling of mindfulness magic:

🐾 When you are walking your dog, take time to be present, enjoying the walk, the peace, nature, appreciating the exercise and thinking about why you are grateful – be it for the sunshine or the green fields or the blessing of having the time to do it. And allow the dog to really enjoy this time, too. Dogs get so much mental stimulation from sniffing (sniffs are like little doggy calling cards – Post-its full of information), so allow them the time to sniff around, rather than whizzing through your walking circuit. Are you a creature of habit with your walks? I am in winter – I hate the cold and the dark mornings and nights and can be guilty of cutting walks down or treading the same pavements night after night. This is uber boring for dogs, however, especially when they aren't free to roam and sniff. Mixing up your walks is great for keeping your dog engaged in walk time and adding enrichment to their lives. They will enjoy the new sights, new smells and their own form of mindful observations. So make it exciting, make it interesting, be engaged and the dog will be engaged, too.

🐾 If it's a nice day, take a moment to sit quietly in nature and just listen. Lead by example. Then your dog will sense your calm and this will calm them, too; they will sit, relishing time of quiet reflection to enjoy their day.

🐾 If you are enjoying dinner, don't worry about things like whether or not you have to put the dog's bed in the washing machine. Instead, concentrate on the taste of the food, feeling grateful for your delicious meal. What does it smell like? What can you hear while you eat? When you take a moment for everything around you *in* that moment, you are being present.

🐾 Meditation is a great activity to do with your dog, as is doggy yoga (more on these on pp. 154 and 158).

🐾 Try simply setting aside a little time out to sit and be still with your dog, perhaps listening to some relaxing music in mutual appreciation.

🐾 Maybe you enjoy reading a good book? Why not read

aloud to your dog? It sounds a little bizarre, but the ebb and flow of your voice can be super relaxing for them. (Just don't let the neighbours see you – they might think you're a bit strange!)

🐾 Have you ever found it tricky to remember something you were doing? Have you ever driven home and not been sure how you got there because you were on autopilot and your mind was elsewhere? Or prepared the dog's dinner, fed them, then had no recollection of having done it? This is because you were multitasking and not focusing your mind. Being present really helps you to remember what you are doing and why. Focusing attention is another great way of adding some mindfulness to your day. Putting your phone away in a drawer and turning off the TV are two steps in the right direction to regain focus on one thing at a time.

🐾 It's said that dogs can't multitask, but they can. They can pee on a bush while scanning the area to see if another dog is watching and then adjust their behaviour accordingly. And they can eat, taste their food and watch their surroundings at the same time. But when they do so, they're not focusing their minds. However, you can help them to focus their attention (my goodness, my dogs could use some help with this, especially my Toy Poodle, who's like a fly in a jar most of the time). In a quiet room, encourage your dog to relax on a mat, then, using your excellent bribery skills and your voice (or a clicker, if you use one), ask them to wait, then reward them with a calm 'Yes' (or a click). Then, as long as they don't move, keep rewarding them, increasing the time between each reward, so they are purely focused on you and hanging on your every word. This short and simple activity trains them while encouraging them to be present and focused, too.

🐾 At feeding time, try thinking thoughts of gratitude for having the means to feed your dog high-quality nutritional foods, for the cosy bed you've provided for them, for the time you spend walking them, making you healthier, for the cuddles and how much joy they bring you with their happy demeanour. Being mindful of all the gratitude you have for these things will surround you with positivity – and I'm such a huge believer that positive attracts positive and reaps big rewards. You will hopefully see transformative effects on both your life and those of the people and animals around you.

There are many hobbies you can do with your dog that have mindful and bonding benefits, from dog yoga to obedience work, and we will cover them in more detail in Chapter 11. There is something for everybody. But, as we've seen, mindfulness can so easily be brought into everyday life, not as a hobby but as a way of thinking – something that can be applied to so many everyday situations, taking up little time but offering rich rewards.

Now that you understand the impact of your lifestyle and the way you are on your dog's mind and behaviour, you can forge ahead with becoming the zen master of dog guardians morning, noon and night. Putting into practice the mindful techniques described in this chapter will make *you* feel so much better, too. It's a win–win for both of you.

6

THE BIG, WIDE WORLD

I'm one of those 'dog mums' who takes a new pup out and about in a sling when they can't walk properly yet. I think it's nice to let them see the big, wide world from a young age and it's great socialisation for them. But I am careful not to bombard them with too much too soon and risk overwhelming them. So it's important to make their introduction a steady one. After all, not all dogs are gregarious, and some prefer to meet people in their own time and approach new situations at a slower pace. It's so exciting having a new dog, and you'll probably want to take them everywhere and show them off to everybody, but you really should allow them a week to settle into their home before you start introducing them to people outside of your household. Particularly when they are little, new things are going to be really tiring for them, so make sure you allow them plenty of time to sleep. They can sleep as much as eighteen to twenty hours a day as puppies – and we all know how important sleep is, so we have to be sure not to deprive them of this, especially when they are growing.

Allow them some time out and quiet time, with short stints when they are relaxed and sleepy on their own. This is a really great way of helping them to feel more confident being alone. When introducing a puppy into a family environment the children will be so excited, so you need to explain to them that they have to respect the puppy, that they need lots of sleep and quiet time and that they shouldn't be played with and cuddled all day. Learn to recognise signs of overtiredness, which may include being super overexcited, zooming around out of control or yawning and trying to settle.

Introducing a puppy to the house is fun – even watching out for signs of needing the toilet! You will find that you become an expert at looking out for those sniffing-and-searching cues.

No stairs for little ones, and you really should be limiting jumping on and off sofas, too. Accidents can happen with puppies on stairs and jumping off furniture and can easily cause both short- and long-term damage to their bodies which aren't yet fully developed.

I love watching my dogs explore a new environment. Even now, on a new walk, they are like meerkats in the car, watching where we are going, and they'll get so excited when we pull into the car park on certain favourite walks. They are so much more aware of familiar places than we may realise; I think my dogs could direct you to most of the parks in my area.

Positive Introductions

Once your new dog has had all their vaccinations (it's best to speak to your local vet about this, as they can advise you on what they think is needed for your dog, but see also p. 45), it's time to explore the big, wide world, but it's important at this point to let them lead the situation and dictate the pace at which this happens, so they are not overwhelmed. Don't forget that these early introductions can shape your dog's entire outlook, so things have to be carefully considered and thought out.

Meeting new people

New introductions, especially in the early days, should take place in a calm environment. If they don't want to approach someone to say hi, don't force it and don't let the person in question just come up to your dog and stroke or interact with them. Instead, chat to the person and explain that your dog is new to meeting people and a little shy; ask them to ignore the dog (which also means no eye contact) and simply let the dog go up to them if they want to for a sniff, with no pressure.

Not all dogs will be leaping over every person and every dog in excitement. With my tribe, I have three very sociable dogs and one who likes to suss you out first. She will be watching your every move, making her mind up, and she responds best to people who are relaxed and don't force themselves on her. She will especially not approach you if you stare at her. Generally, she will just watch the others say hi and isn't at all fussed about saying hello herself. This is simply her character; she's a one-woman dog and, to be honest, she just thinks I'm the best and all she needs in her life!

As I've said previously, every dog is unique, so tune in to your dog's spirit, try to read situations and gauge how they are feeling. (This goes back to you being the zen master of dogs again . . .) Your dog will thank you for your insight and feel secure in your presence. But don't reward them for being shy or stand-offish. Rather, offer them calm reassurance or just let them take a step back and distract them by doing something else.

Travel and transport

There are many ways of getting about with a dog, and each comes with different perks and challenges.

Travel by car

It's important that from the moment you collect your dog they get used to being in a car, even if you don't own one. Why? Because you never know when you may need to pop your dog in one – maybe to get to a new walk or for a vet visit. It needn't be traumatic, but for lots of puppies the first time they are in a car is when they leave their mama, and they are not taken out for rides much after that, so they can end up associating the car with something they don't want to do.

I have had a couple of litters over the years (I'm not a breeder but, as I show dogs, I may have a litter to keep their breed lines going and to keep one myself). These puppies are popped in the car regularly from a young age, for vet visits, but also for an aimless, steady ride around the block. I put a large, strong crate in my boot and away we go. In my opinion, this early regular car travel (from the age of less than eight weeks) is the reason why none of my dogs suffers with either travel sickness or car anxiety. Travelling in the car should be as natural as popping into the garden. And they look so sweet peering out at the passing countryside.

But what if you have rescued a dog or have one that already suffers with car anxiety and sickness?

As with any new training, you need to start slow. Strip things right back, starting with putting your dog on a lead and walking them near the car. Don't get too close – start far away – and reward them for acknowledging the car or walking near it. Be calm and offer reassurance. Next, very gradually, build up to the point where you are opening and closing the car doors, then reward. After a week of doing this every day, your dog may be ready to be inside the car. Allow them to get in, sit with them and reassure them, either playing with them or offering some positive interactions or food rewards.

From this point, you want to build up from just getting

in and out of the vehicle to turning it on and walking past it, then sitting in the parked vehicle when it's running, then travelling literally 50m and back and so on. It takes time to reverse a negative association, and you have to be careful not to push the dog too far too fast, as that could undo the work you've done so far.

Think about where they sit in the vehicle, too. The boot can be scary if they can't look out easily and may also be too bouncy. When I first take my dogs in the car, I use the back seats. It's less bouncy there and they can still be near us.

For a new puppy, someone should snuggle the puppy on their first journey in the back seat. Bring blankets, too, and I would hope the dog's breeder gives you something that smells of Mum to offer as a comforter.

Then it's all about exposure. Take the dog out as often as possible in the car, with someone present to hold them initially. Make it a positive experience – not just going to the vet for their vaccinations. Puppies are like sponges, so it's important to introduce them to all these new experiences as young and as often as possible.

I love travelling with my dogs. We have been to the south of France, both ends of the United Kingdom, including stunning places like the Lake District. We have a full car, especially as the children always travel with everything but the kitchen sink. We all love our adventures, and it brings me so much joy to see the happiness in all the others – both two- and four-legged. Plus, it's wonderful bonding time, relaxing and enjoying our days together.

Introducing your dog to a bus
As much as I believe we should all be leaving our cars at home and using public transport more, I'm guilty of not using it to its full potential. However, my children always enjoy the novelty of a bus journey, and we'll bring a dog along, too, for the experience. That way, the bus journey

turns into a fun adventure with the gang and my dog gets some new stimulation, where they are all wide-eyed and full of that puppy-like inquisitiveness.

It can be easy to underestimate how scary a big, rattling busy bus can be to a dog. So introducing them slowly is important to prevent them from becoming fearful. Ensure that you have with you lots of big-value treats, chews and their favourite snuggle toy for comfort, as well as offering lots of encouragement (and the same applies when you are introducing any form of transport, be it a bus or train, taxi or boat).

Start by moving slowly near the bus stop, where the noises and volume of people increase. Check in with them – are they comfortable? It's important not to bombard them by rushing straight into the situation – whether it's a bus stop or bus station – which can be an assault on the senses and 'flood' them. This could mean that the first few times you try and you realise your dog isn't comfortable, you'll have to remove them from the situation before they become very anxious.

Make sure your first journey is a short one – a hop-on-hop-off trip. If you have other dogs or a friend with a dog that happily uses public transport, it's a good idea to travel together, as dogs do look to their friends for support and guidance in new situations and often copy behaviours.

After they have mastered their first few trips, you can increase journey time and reduce the number of treats as they feel more and more confident.

Travel by train

The train is a comfortable way of travelling with a dog. It's a smooth journey and they will be close to you for the duration, so the majority of their training and encouragement will need to focus on the busy station, embarking and disembarking, finding an appropriate place for their 'rest break' and being comfortable around strangers in the carriage.

For a peaceful journey, make sure you plan it in advance and, if possible, tire them out before you set off. With smaller, 'liftable' dogs, I carry them on and off the train; and I use treats to coax larger dogs over the threshold, ensuring they are always in a secure harness or lead and I have full control of them.

Trains (and any form of public transport) can be daunting for dogs who are 'new-person shy'. Keep a check that strangers don't lunge at them for a stroke and instead inform them that your dog is shy, that they should not stare at them and let them have their space. With this in mind, find the quietest carriage possible, where you can sit close to them and reassure them.

Road sense

With busy roads everywhere, it would be unusual for a dog not to come close to a stream of traffic at some point in their life, and the roadside is not the place for a freaking-out dog who could potentially slip their collar.

A positive introduction to a road is important, especially for smaller breeds – it must be so daunting for them being near all those speeding steel boxes on wheels. Whatever must they think? Breeds like the Border Collie can have a real prey drive (an instinctive tendency to find and pursue prey) when it comes to cars, chasing and getting agitated by traffic. I've seen this become a dangerous set-in behaviour in many a Collie-type. So when it comes to road sense, it's ideal, again, to start them young and slowly.

Start on a quiet road, find a bench and relax. Make sure you have their reward to hand – their special treat or favourite toy – and when a car approaches, allow them to watch, take in what's happening and reward the behaviour that you want to see. Then, gradually build them up to walking on a slightly busier road, encouraging and rewarding them, and, when you feel they aren't fazed by the moving traffic, you can progress to walking alongside busier and busier roads. Just take it slow.

If your dog takes a backwards step and becomes fearful or overwhelmed, don't be put off. Just go back to the beginning, keeping them away from busier roads, and work again through the slow introduction, using plenty of treats and soothing encouragement.

When you actually need to cross over the road, ideally find a proper crossing point. Ask your dog to sit beside you and wait there until it's safe to cross over. Then reward and praise them for being such a clever sausage.

Livestock training

If, like me, you enjoy the beautiful countryside and spending weekends donning your walking boots and getting out into the great outdoors, you'll need to think about doing some livestock training.

I love a circular walk, but often public rights of way cross farmers' fields and, at certain times of the year, these are filled with sheep or cattle.

When entering a field with livestock, dogs should remain on a lead at all times. In fact, when entering any field at all, they should be on a lead because sometimes the livestock may gather over the brow of a hill or in a corner where you may not be able to see them straight away.

I'll be straight with you: I'm petrified of cows. Well, more specifically, cows on the loose in fields – because I don't actually mind cows per se, having spent many years in Austria looking after them, feeding calves and tracking them in the mountains with some family friends who have a farm out there. My real issue is with British cows and is due to the number of times I've been chased, throwing myself over walls and stiles, running as fast as my legs could carry me, despite having given them a wide berth. I can laugh about it now . . . a little . . . but honestly, it's left this terrible anxiety in me. And the fact that I know of two people who have been hospitalised following a cow trample hasn't helped! So I try to dodge the cow situation as much as possible, even considering walking the wrong way just to avoid them.

Having said all that, dogs are clever when it comes to picking up on our emotions, so I have to work really hard when entering a field of cows, just to keep my anxiety under wraps. That tighter hold of the lead, the increased intake of breath, that worried expression, the way we flare our nostrils when stressed, even the smell of stress on our breath – they are so in tune with us and can sense our fear. And I don't want my irrational (or possibly rational) fear to impact my dogs' behaviour, so that they become fearful or too protective.

We need our dogs to be calm and relaxed around livestock, so early introductions are important, especially with those breeds who inherently want to chase sheep or cattle, particularly when they are running. Being chased by a dog can be so stressful for sheep that they can even abort their unborn lambs; plus, it also runs the risk of the farmer shooting the dog (which they are within their rights to do here in the UK if a dog is worrying their animals and out of control). So it's doubly important to train dogs around livestock – for the sake of the other animals as well as their own.

Start from far away, across the other side of a field and behind the fencing. Allow your dog to look at the livestock and have your high-value reward on hand, treating them only when they look away and look at you. You may also add a 'good'. Next, steadily move towards the livestock, with a relaxed lead, gauging the dog's body language – you want to see a relaxed dog here. They can be interested and looking at the livestock, but should not show any signs of aggression, lunging, barking or being fixated on them. Instead, they should just calmly check them out, acknowledging them, but not getting hyped up. And again, when they are uninterested, reward.

The progression of this process really does hinge on your ability to read your dog's body language and to see how you feel they are responding to the livestock. Slow and steady wins the race, as they say.

If you need to cross a field with livestock in it, give them as wide a berth as you possibly can and ensure you aren't walking through the middle of a herd (you could be separating a mother from her young, which could cause her to be defensive). If a cow approaches you, don't panic – just very calmly walk away. But if your dog is being chased or charged at, let go of their lead and let them run. Most dogs can outrun a cow, whereas we can't.

A calm and relaxed dog equals a happy you, and you really will find that through all this hard work in the early years you will reap the rewards for the rest of your journey together. Yes, training is time consuming, but the more you put in, the more you get out: fast forward a couple of years and whenever you need to hop on a train or bus or cross a busy road or a field of livestock, your dog will already have done this, processed it with that calm early training and socialisation and it will just be another day of fun-filled adventures.

Doggy Decorum

Being a decent dog guardian is about ensuring that you both have good etiquette and that you can co-exist with those around you without being a nuisance or disturbance.

Good dog protocol means, among other things, *not* just bagging your dog's poop and leaving it lying around in public, but taking it away with you. It means *not* being completely unaware of what your dog is doing at the local park while you are on your phone, having a debrief with your bestie. It means *not* allowing your bouncy dog to jump up on strangers, ignoring signage that states dogs must be kept on leads. And it means *not* allowing your dog to pee all over other people's property. (For more on dog etiquette and how to be a good and responsible guardian, see p. 83–95.)

Dog Chat

Dog people love to chat with fellow dog people. We have a mutual love and appreciation for our fuzz heads. I love a bit of dog chat more than my husband does – he can sometimes be a bit dogged out! (Did he know what he was letting himself in for marrying me?) I mean, he did have a dog of his own when we met, but I take my love of dogs to the next level: I work with them all day long, live with them 24/7 and, on a weekend, I'll either be showing my dogs, walking them or cleaning up after them. Sweet heaven, right? But not for everyone.

Engaging in dog chat is a great way of socialising your new dog and meeting and engaging with people in your neighbourhood. My dogs are a conversation starter because you don't see many Poodles – especially not a pack of them in show coats – so I get stopped quite a lot, and it's so nice taking the time to chat with strangers and letting our dogs greet each other.

I will rarely walk past a fellow walker without engaging. Which is funny, isn't it? Because generally, we tend to walk head down when we're out and about, rarely acknowledging passers-by. But stick us on a dog walk with a lead in our hands and, all of a sudden, we are transformed into chatty, cheery ambassadors for humankind.

Dog chat is a way of being present, truly appreciating your dog walk, your time with your dog and the great outdoors. Make a point of turning off your devices, putting the headphones back in your pocket and looking around. Make it your mission to say hello to every passer-by.

One way of brightening someone else's day is by paying a compliment. I love it when someone compliments my pooches. It makes me feel so proud, lightening my mood, and, in turn, the happiness is spread around, as I've appreciated the compliment and will pass it on. I think that's something we can often forget about ourselves – that we are all about energy, feeding on it just as dogs do. Whether it's with our loved ones, our work mates or the small interactions we have with strangers, it all makes a difference to the energy we want to put out there, how we want to feel and how we make others feel, too. Apart from brightening your walk, stopping for these interactions is also a great opportunity for different dogs to mix for longer than a passing hello and a quick sniff. Dogs generally like to spend time with their own species – running around together, peeing on top of each other's pee – and it will tire their minds and their bodies out more than a solo walk. They could meet a really fun new bestie, and this can lead to you having new walking buddies, too, enriching the experience for both you and your dog.

Sensory Walking

I don't have a set routine. With two small children, a pack of dogs and both myself and my husband being self-employed, my days are hectic and each one is different. Some people like a routine, but I have found that the variety in our days and the no-structure ethos just works for our home and our dogs. It means that they're not standing around at 4.30, waiting for their meal, for example; they know it's coming, but it could be at 4 or 5pm. And they don't start howling if we don't come downstairs at 6am; they know we might not be down until 7am. Variety is key – and that applies to their exercise, too.

I live in a popular dog-walking spot, as my house overlooks a park. I see the same people, following the same routine with the same walk every day at the same time. And I think, How boring! Boring for them, but also mega boring for their dogs, the only perk of their walks being the possibility that another dog may come around the corner because, by now, they have sniffed every smell there is to sniff. (This, by the way, can cause overarousal when they do meet another dog because they are so bored by that point.)

Including different walking locations is so important for your dog's introduction to the big, wide world and all it has in it – you are expanding their mind and adding such enrichment. There are many different types of walks to discover, so try them all. Here are some examples:

🐾 **Woodland** It's dark and mysterious, and you can't see too far ahead through all the trees; and there are new noises everywhere, like cracking twigs and calling birds. There is often the smell of wild garlic and rotting wood and an uneven terrain.

🐾 **Moorland** This tends to be wild and windy with bouncy heather and uneven trails. The ground birds appear from nowhere and there often isn't a soul to be seen. It smells fresh with the aroma of heather and peat.

🐾 **Lakeside walks** The sounds of geese fill the air, the paths are easier to walk, often gravelly and busy with people from all walks of life.

🐾 **The seaside** This is a treat for my dogs. The sounds of seagulls and crashing waves, sandy beaches where they can run around with washed-up seaweed or an old fishing rope. There is the smell of the salty sea air and the mouth-watering scent of fish and chips.

🐾 **Town** A lovely place to meet lots of new people, all eager to greet a dog. There's the bustle of shoppers pounding the pavements, the sounds of cars and buses, people chatting and the scents of restaurants and coffee shops.

🐾 **Parkland** Here, your dog can run after their ball in big, open spaces, play with their dog pals, sniff all the heavily marked trees or go for a rummage in the hedges. It smells of cut grass and morning dew.

If you don't know where to start, there may be an online group in your area for dog walkers and you could ask their advice; or pop in the car and go on an expedition – perhaps into the countryside. The UK has some of the most gorgeous countryside, meaning new and exciting places for your dog. And a woodland is so much more thrilling for them than a local field. So get out there and start exploring.

A long time ago, someone told me about a very old-school way of looking at dog walking, whereby you are the pack leader – it's *your* walk – and the dog is only allowed two pee stops and one for poop. You walk tall and with confidence (well, the confidence thing still applies) and don't allow your dog to stop and sniff around. That's so wrong because dogs learn so much from sniffing, and preventing them from exploring in this way – essentially, exhibiting normal canine behaviour – is storing up stress and anxiety for them in the future. That's why sensory walking is so important.

A sensory walk is just what it says on the tin – a walk that will really stimulate the senses. Why not try a little experiment? First, take your dog for their evening walk in your regular spot and monitor their behaviour. Then, on another evening, take them on a new woodland walk for the same length of time as the previous one, and observe any differences. You may notice afterwards that they settle quicker and for longer at home, enjoy longer sleeps and are a lot calmer and more content. The stimulation from these more exciting new walks, where they have the time and freedom to roam, sniff and explore, is so much more tiring for them than that boring turn around a field. Whether I am walking a puppy or an older dog, I am always looking for new places to show them, new adventures and days out.

Consistently introducing your dog to new things in the big, wide world will have such a positive impact on their mental health. It will help any issues you may have with their behaviour and they will be much calmer to live with. Variety is the spice of life! But if it's a rubbish day, or you can't get out for whatever reason, there are other ways you can work their minds by turning your home into a new and interesting place for them:

- Try creating a sensory trail in your garden, using upturned flowerpots with things hidden under them.

- Ask your dog to sit in front of you indoors, then, using three cups, pop a treat under one of them and, like a magician, mix them up to see if they can find the right one straight away.

- As long as your dog isn't anxious, hide and seek can be fun.

- Grab an old towel, lay it flat and then roll it up into a sausage, rolling some treats into it as you go along.

- I love to make use of the mountains of recycling we create – try using toilet-roll tubes to hide treats in, for example; or my big girlie loved a crunchy plastic bottle to play with (I pop treats inside and cut small holes so they have to roll the bottle around to get them out).

- Use old, tatty clothes to tie into knots and create your own tug toys.

- Get your children to build a dog-house den out of some old cardboard boxes.

With lots of these activities, you can get the whole family involved. It's great fun when giggling children hide under their bed with pooch! The ideas are endless, but just make sure that the dog is supervised at all times. And let dogs be dogs; their mental health and overall wellbeing will thank you for it.

Mindful tip

We are only human, but when we are introducing new things and settling in a new dog, we really need to keep a check on our own energy and on our dogs'. So whatever your day has been like, try to reset at the door; or perhaps sit in your car for five minutes and listen to a favourite song or practise a three-four-five breathing technique (see p. 158). Hopefully, this will help you to realign yourself, not just for your own benefit, but for those around you, too – including your dog.

WALKERS' ETIQUETTE

There is an unspoken walkers' etiquette that you'll need to get to grips with. Owning a dog is fraught with mishaps and learning curves, so you should expect to make some blunders; but being aware of some ground rules will help you to avoid any (or at least some) faux pas. Here's my run-down of walkers' etiquette – how to be thoughtful when out and about and how to make it the most peaceful and mindful experience possible.

Rule number 1: always pick up after your dog
It should be second nature when you are heading out to grab a dog-poo bag: lead, poo bag, ready. I find the dispensers attached to the lead are handy if you are likely to forget to take bags, but the pockets of every coat I own seem to be bursting with them, too. And I also keep a supply in the boot of my car and in the side pocket of my handbag. It would literally be my worst nightmare if I was out and caught short. I would be so embarrassed.

Rule number 2: pay attention
Be present on your walk. It's not just about being there for your dog and spending quality time with them, but also about being aware of your surroundings, possible dangers and potentially sticky situations. You know your dog: perhaps they have a vendetta against cats or cars; or perhaps they can be over the top when meeting other dogs who could be on the lead. There are so many tricky scenarios that could play out on a walk, so you need to be alert

to your surroundings and ahead of the game at all times.

Rule number 3: on and off the lead
If another dog is on the lead, it's wrong to let your dog who is off the lead approach them. So if your dog doesn't have bomb-proof recall, you need to put them on a lead and keep them under control. Equally, if you have a dog in training or an elderly dog on the lead, then be aware of those off the lead, especially those who are seemingly out of control. And if you have an aggressive dog, you do have a duty of care to protect those around you – so it would be silly, in my view, to walk them in a popular dog-walking area.

Remember, dogs aren't robots and, although your recall may be 99 per cent there, they have their own minds and it's still a possibility that they may approach a leaded dog. Leads that are colour-coded and marked with 'nervous' or such like are great. I always look twice if I see a yellow lead. Here's a little guide to what the various colours signify:

Yellow: I'm nervous, please give me space
Red: caution, I just want space
Green: I'm friendly; hello!
Orange: I like people; I don't like other dogs
White: I can't hear you or I can't see you; I'm deaf and/or blind
Blue: I'm in training/I'm learning something new, for work
Purple: don't feed me

Rule number 4: respect others (including dogs)

Not everyone likes dogs – shocking, I know; but seriously, some people have a genuine fear, maybe because of a bad experience (my mum was timid around unknown dogs, as she was chased as a small girl riding her bike and a dog got her by the ankle; I mean, that's pretty terrifying for anyone). So we should be aware that not everyone is happy and comfortable with dogs in their space, and it's always polite to ask, 'Is it ok if I sit here with my dog?' or, 'Is it ok if I bring my dog in here?' It's a fabulous dog parent who really thinks about everyone around them.

We should respect a dog's space, too. I so often see people forcing themselves on dogs (even unknown ones), not picking up on their cues for space, not reading their body language. Or a dog's custodian might be having a chat with someone who's admiring the dog, and just thrust the wee thing on them. As stunning or delightful as these dogs may be, they don't all want love and cuddles all the time.

Two of my dogs go gaga for an ounce of affection from anyone, be it the postie, the window cleaner . . . they are just bonkers, craving all the looks and tickles. Another one, however, likes to figure you out a little first, while another is absolutely 100 per cent for me and my family only and, although she would tolerate a stranger touching her, she certainly wouldn't invite it.

We need to respect a dog's wishes and their personality, allowing them to have their space and approach you on their own terms if they so wish.

On the subject of respect, something that grinds my gears is dog custodians who love their own dog so much but have a complete lack of respect for other animals – cats in particular. I've heard people winding up their dogs about cats, encouraging a chase instinct in them. I just don't get it, and it's something I have to speak out about if I hear it: how would they feel if it was their dog being chased down by someone's bigger pet? All animals deserve respect. So think like a Buddhist, and treat all how you would like to be treated. (FYI, I'm a spider rescuer, even a fly rescuer – never a squasher.)

Rule number 5: respect others' property

Only a few weeks ago, I was wandering through a pet shop and saw a chap shopping with a large dog in tow. Walking behind him, I observed the dog lifting his leg on every corner of the aisle, spraying stock, food and soft toys in his path. I called the man out, explaining that people would pick those products up, and it was soiled stock. And I told the shop assistants, who said they see this on a daily basis. I just don't get it – if you know your dog is a marker, why on earth would you take them somewhere like that? We need to be respectful of people's property – the kind of dog guardians that 'non-doggy' folk think are pretty cool and make dog care look easy.

I've been to lots of parks where there are ponds or lakes, nesting birds and such like, and big signs requesting that dogs are kept on leads (and why). Yet nearly every time, I will see at least one dog swimming or roaming through the undergrowth. Dogs can't read, so it's not their fault, but their guardians have no respect for the space they're in. What if we all did that? They're simply not thinking about the bigger picture.

We have a duty of care as our dogs' guardians and

as members of society to help our animals to respect others' property; and we too must respect the world we live in, cleaning up after our dogs and respecting the wishes of others.

Being in Tune With Your Dog

Dogs are great readers of energy. Of course, what you say and how you act are important, but they will always be reading and picking up on your energy, too. So whatever you introduce your dog to or however you wish them to behave, think about your own energy. For example, if you are feeling really stressed while walking them, you may be holding their lead tighter and shorter than normal and they will pick up on this and become stressed, too, wondering why you are so tense and whether there is something worrying coming up around the next corner. Or if you come in from work after a particularly stressful day, and your dog excitedly greets you as they usually do but your energy is negative, stressed and anxious, they will pick up on this straight away. They won't understand why you feel this way, but it will make them worried and anxious, too. Or perhaps you are on the bus together and someone really annoys you; you may sit there feeling wound up, and your dog will pick up on this, but they won't understand why you are cross – all they will register is that you are out of sorts and that will rub off on them.

The world is big, noisy and chaotic, so remember to take things slowly and calmly!

7

FEEDING THE BODY – DIET, NUTRITION . . . AND WASTE

Dogs can't make choices, so we must make careful and ethical ones for them. Choosing your dog's food involves three main considerations: nutritional value, what you can afford and the environmental impact that food has on the planet.

You Are What You Eat

I'm no nutritionist, but I have been around dogs long enough to know the basics. So while this section isn't going to be an in-depth look at the different nutrients and what they do, I am going to say something I have harped on for years: that what you put into a dog, you get out of them.

Am I wrong for judging that person with the big diamond ring and designer handbag picking up the budget food in the supermarket pet aisle? I understand that quality food can be pricey, but I just implore you to buy the best food that your pocket will allow (and no, that doesn't mean you can still have your ten pints down the pub and feed your pet multicoloured biscuits of utter rubbish). And in any case, it's almost a false economy buying the cheap grain-filled nutritionally poor dog food because they need twice as much of it to thrive, and their waste out the other end is never-ending; not to mention the head fog the dog gets from eating that stuff.

Dos and Don'ts

Let's go back to basics: what can't your dog eat?

There is so much contraband in your home that you may not realise is harmful for your dog – not just irritants, but also dangerous.

My darling Dobermann was about three years old when she raided my mum's compost heap, looking for a sneaky snack. We didn't even know she had done so, until after she got seriously ill. The little scavenger had eaten a corn-on-the-cob husk – whole! We realised when she suddenly became so unwell that we took her to the vet, who X-rayed her and found an obstruction. By this point, it had been inside her a while, blocking her up. Several thousands of pounds and operations later, she survived, but she lost some of her intestine as a result. Luckily, not her life – although it was close.

As much as we try to keep harmful foods away from our dogs, there is always that ninja pooch that does what no other dog has done before, raiding a bin or opening a cupboard. So prepare for a ninja dog as much as you can. As discussed earlier (see p. 25), you need to keep bins secure and out of the way (inside a cupboard or with a lid that's difficult for a dog to open). Be especially careful around Christmas and Easter, when there will be lots of nuts, treats, cake and chocs around. (For more on food no-nos, see p. 86.) If you are having a party with food and drink, I would pop your dog away somewhere safe until it's all been cleared away. (I have young children who carry snacks around with them, and they are prone to dropping as many as they consume, so, again, it's wise to pop your dog in the garden or another room while kids are snacking.) And when you are busy preparing dinner, as mentioned earlier, don't leave your roast chicken in plain sight when you have to pop to the loo or elsewhere – instead, leave it in the oven or at the back of your worktop.

Having a dog around means adopting a what-if mentality. Try to risk assess your space as far as possible – it's better to be safe than sorry.

Choosing the right diet

It's easy to get sucked in by savvy sales and cute packaging, but it's what's inside that packaging that matters. So whether you decide to feed a raw diet or pre-made wet or dry food, always look at the ingredients. There are a few websites that can help you make a good choice if you are unsure (search for comparison sites or see Resources, p.248), but in essence, ingredients are listed on packaging in order of quantity, so if the first is a protein source, that's great; if it's a filler or grain, then return it to the shelf (cereal, whole wheat, flaked wheat, maize, meat and animal derivatives, vegetable derivatives, meat and bone meal are the main ones to avoid; they are what we would call 'fillers' – they fill the dog up, but offer poor nutritional value):

🐾 Meat and animal derivatives are a by-product from the human food chain. They are safe for a dog to consume but are cheap and of poor quality – essentially, they are the bits that cannot be sold in the butchers (udders, lungs, spleen, heart, beaks and hooves).

PUPPY NUTRITION

Puppies grow at an astonishing rate, reaching adulthood at around a year old. These little growing machines need so much nutritional support to ensure they reach their healthiest, most gorgeous potential and are able to stave off illnesses such as diabetes, pancreatitis and skin and fur conditions.

I find a diverse range of foods is great. If you feed your little one just one type of food morning, noon and night, then when you decide to add in something different it can upset their delicate tummies. My puppies are all fed a variety of foods – raw or cooked human-grade and kibble. Getting their bodies used to this mixed diet from a young age helps their digestive systems.

A raw diet usually contains a combination of raw meat, muscle meat, organ meats such as liver, tripe and kidneys, raw bones whole or ground and other uncooked ingredients like vegetables, often with added vitamins and minerals, too. This type of food is based on the diet of your dog's wild ancestors. There are so many options, but balance is the key, and they must get all the nutrients and minerals they need to thrive. So now is not the time (actually, it never is in my book) to scrimp on your food choices.

Puppies can take longer to eat their dinner so, to avoid food theft, I feed my pups in a crate. This reinforces their love of their den – their space – and they dive in when the bowls emerge and meal preparation starts, waiting expectantly for their supper. I leave them in there for five minutes, then retrieve any unwanted food. If you only have one dog in the house and they walk away from their dinner bowl, lift it up after five minutes and return it to them at lunch time. Avoid getting into the habit of letting them graze like a cat, as mealtimes then won't be something to look forward to, as food is on tap whenever they fancy. This also makes it harder to monitor weight loss or gain.

🐾 Vegetable derivatives are, again, the by-products from the human food chain – a mixture of poor-quality veg not fit for human consumption.

🐾 Meat and bone meal is a product from the meat-rendering industry made from mammal tissues, some bone, connecting tissues and offal – again, the bits that aren't fit for human consumption. It's cooked at extremely high temperatures and then dehydrated down into a brown powder.

🐾 Vegetable protein extracts are vegetable sources from which the nutrients have been chemically extracted – a cheap way of adding vegetable protein to foods.

The primary ingredients you should look for are fresh chicken, salmon, lamb and turkey. Other good ingredients include sweet potatoes, carrots, seaweed, salmon oil, dried cranberries, chicory root, parsley, lentils and flaxseed.

I like to choose foods in which every ingredient is something that I have actually heard of and would eat myself. Raw feeding is popular now, and you can give your dog a complete balanced diet this way, feeding as nature intended.

Make sure you buy a quality raw diet, checking ingredients, as described above. Raw foods are specifically prepared and frozen down, using high human-grade meat, bone and vegetables. It's important to be safe when feeding any meat or fish, just as you would be preparing your own meat meals (assuming you are not vegetarian), so keep your prep area clean both before and afterwards, wash bowls out immediately following their dinner and don't let your dog lick you straight after a meal.

Often, a dog's raw food comprises tripe. It's stinky stuff and, while dogs love it, it taints other foods it comes into contact with, so keep it as far away in your freezer from your own food as possible.

Don't be put off raw as a choice of feeding due to the freezing, prep and cleaning-up issues. It's easy to get into a routine of pulling out tomorrow's food when you feed your dogs their evening meal and I am always prepared with environmentally friendly antibacterial spray, while their bowls just go in the dishwasher. You can also use raw-dog-food delivery services that will come every week or every fortnight, if you don't have much freezer space.

A new type of dog food on the market is gently cooked dog food. This comprises the ingredients from a high-quality raw complete food that have been gently cooked and then quickly frozen down without the need for any nasty preservatives. I have tried this food with my fusspots and they absolutely love it.

Kibble is an easier way of feeding your dog, and there are some fabulous ones out there, containing high levels of protein. And what's more, you will recognise all the ingredients on the packaging – bonus!

You can even buy insect-based high-protein foods for your dog now. They don't smell like worms, nor do they have hairy cricket legs poking out of them. My dogs have eaten insect-based protein and loved it – and I do have fussy

FOOD SUPPLEMENTS

You may be feeding your pooch the best-quality diet, but you might want to consider supplements, too. Many companies now specialise in supplements specifically for dogs, and I have listed here the most popular ones and their benefits for our beloved dogs.

🐾 **Omega oil/fish oils** Thought to help skin allergies, as well as improve coat quality and shine. The *American Journal of Veterinary Research* suggests that fish oils also reduce inflammation, and many pet owners use them for this purpose.[2]

🐾 **Glucosamine** Probably the most popular supplement, glucosamine is an amino sugar, found naturally around joints. Many believe that it is an effective supplement to help dogs who are suffering from the effects of arthritis and to aid mobility and relieve joint pain in older dogs.

🐾 **Probiotics** Just as we have seen an increase in the use of probiotics in humans, we have also seen an increase in their use for our dogs. Probiotics live naturally in the body, aiding digestion and intestinal health. This is particularly important after a dose of antibiotics; they strip the dog's gut of good and bad bacteria alike, so it's important we replenish the good ones. They can be found in capsule or powder form, in yoghurts and in chews.

2 https://avmajournals.avma.org/view/journals/ajvr/69/4/ajvr.69.4.486.xml

> 🐾 **Antioxidants** Ageing can bring with it memory loss and cognitive dysfunction, but antioxidants can counteract some of these effects. Found in vitamins, including C and E, they protect the body from cell damage. Co-enzyme Q10 for dogs is another natural source of antioxidants.

poodles. The unique selling point of these foods is that they are much kinder to the environment (they don't need as much water to produce) and some brands are the world's first sustainable dog foods. As such, they are a great option if you are interested in helping the environment or you are a vegan or vegetarian. You'll be feeding with ease, while giving them the nutrients they need.

How to feed

I don't let my dogs graze like cats, because it means I can't monitor their intake, especially in a multi-dog household. Plus, they don't have the same appetite for mealtimes if the food is there all the time. Having said that, I never had a problem with food being left out when I had Dobermanns, and I remember my grandad's Labradors would literally inhale their food, like industrial vacuum cleaners. They would eat everything in sight, probably throw it up due to the sheer volume and then eat that, too! But small Poodles are different, and they are generally known to be fussy eaters.

I feed my dogs separately. I have to because my gluttonous elderly Poodle (a Labrador in Poodle clothing) hovers around like a vulture, waiting to ensure every dog's bowl is immaculately licked clean.

I'm lucky that there aren't any arguments over food in my house, but I attribute that to my dogs having respect for one another and allowing the slower eaters to feed in a safe space. With four dogs, all with different quirks and requirements, I have designated places where they like to eat. I have a crate in my utility where I put the slowest feeder with her food – she gallops in at mealtimes and sits and waits. Then the gobbler and the food thief eat together in my kitchen or outside. I give them their dinners to eat in peace. If, after ten minutes, their food hasn't been eaten, I take it away. And if I notice that one of the picky poodles hasn't eaten at all, I will offer them something on their own, away from the prying eyes of the pack.

I feed my adult dogs twice a day and the puppies more often, depending on their age. And if I am heading out or am busy working, they get a dried fish skin or something yummy like that. You should have received lots of helpful advice on how frequently to feed your puppy from their breeder or rescue centre, but here is a rough guide:

- 🐾 Two–four months: four times a day, at evenly spread intervals during waking hours

- 🐾 Four–six months: three times a day – breakfast, lunch and dinner

- 🐾 Six months: twice a day (depending on breed and weight)

On dry days, a great way of feeding your dog and adding enrichment to the experience is to scatter feed – you literally scatter their food all over the garden. This stretches out dinner time and gives them a fun and rewarding activity, too. I love scatter feeding – it encourages dogs to demonstrate their natural behaviour as they sniff out their food.

A dog's nose is a powerful tool and sniffing tires them out mentally, as they have to analyse every scent.

You can scatter feed inside your home, too, although I don't do this (call me house proud). But I do love a snuffle mat or a puzzle feeder. A snuffle mat is a flat mat covered in rags of material; you scatter food into it and the dogs have to snuffle around to find it. Puzzle feeders come in many different shapes and sizes with compartments that hold food and can be manipulated in different ways to release it.

I have loads of puzzle feeders. My dogs love them, and the little geniuses are pretty good at using them, too. I'm just laughing as I remember when I got my first puzzle feeder many years ago. My Poodles would spend ages figuring the game out, finding the treats and working on their problem solving, whereas my Dobermann girl would just batter it with her paws and flip it, then stand on it and eat all the treats. That was her way of showing us she was of a higher intelligence!

A healthy weight

With feeding in mind, this is a good place to talk about weight. I work with dogs every day and, while many are a fabulous weight, I see loads that are too heavy. In fact, there is currently an obesity epidemic.

Dogs who are neutered and spayed seem to be at increased risk of this problem, as do middle-aged dogs. The Royal Veterinary College has found that certain breeds are predisposed to carrying excess weight, too and these include the Pug, Springer Spaniel, Golden Retriever, Labrador and the Beagle.

Why is it so important that dogs maintain their optimum weight? Well, excess weight, as we know with people, carries many health and lifestyle implications. But with dogs, we have to be doubly conscious of it, because their health and weight are our responsibility. We eat what we fancy and lead the lifestyle we choose and the repercussions of that – good or bad – are down to us. But we are the guardians of these precious creatures so, regardless of whether they are eight weeks or eight years old, their health and food habits should always be something we concern ourselves with.

Excess weight has a negative impact on a dog's quality of life, putting their little legs and joints under a lot more strain, so that they won't enjoy their walks as much and can't run as fast, feeling the wind in their ears. Obesity also carries with it a much greater risk of heart disease, some types of cancer and diabetes to name a few, potentially shortening lifespan.

I urge you to develop healthy feeding habits for your dogs, being careful with the amount you are feeding them. Start with the feeding guide on their food's packaging, but bear in mind this is a rough guide; for example, a dog who exercises a lot will burn off loads more food; and some dogs have a faster or slower metabolism. Next, try looking at your dog from above: do they look more of an oval or rotund shape? From the side, does their tummy sag or look oval, in line with their rib cage. Or does it stick out even further? Have a feel for their ribs – if they aren't extremely prominent and you can't easily feel them, there is too much fat in the way. Dogs will store fat in fat pads, too – these can be between the front legs, at the top of the hips and the base of the tail. If you notice any of these things, they could be overweight. If you are unsure, ask your vet what they think about their current weight. Then increase or decrease food accordingly, gradually, over time, until you have reached your dog's perfect feeding regime.

Also, avoid fatty treats (some of the dental chews on the market are so bad for them – they may as well be eating a double cheeseburger before bed) and instead, swap out for healthier alternatives, such as pre-packed air-dried meat or fish or foods found at home, such as watermelon, peas and banana or perhaps a crunchy carrot.

We each have a responsibility to take care of our environment, and, as the custodians of our precious pooches, we should be making considered choices that benefit both them and the space around us. We can all adopt eco-friendly habits, making thoughtful purchases that go beyond meeting their initial needs. I have a tattoo on my hand – it is a Buddhist mantra about nurturing nature. Buddha taught that we all need to live in harmony with nature; he understood that we rely on nature so much and nature relies on us, too. It's all about karma and, whether you are religious, spiritual or a non-believer, it's still a beautiful way to conduct your life.

So, beyond their feeding regime, how else can we apply this mindset to living with a dog?

Poop Disposal

This is an important issue we face as dog custodians. After figuring out what we are putting into their bodies to fuel them, it has to come back out!

If you could pile up the mountain of bagged poop your dog creates just in a year, it would be astonishing; and given that their bottom waste is organic matter, after all, wrapping it in plastic, thereby preventing its decomposition, is pretty crazy. So although when we are out and about we do have to collect our dogs' dos in something, using biodegradable bags at least means the wrapping will break down much quicker compared to normal plastic ones, which can take hundreds, even thousands of years to decompose.

We should all be environmentally aware when it comes to what we are purchasing and disposing of. Not all biodegradable bags are equal. Some are labelled 'biodegradable' but will still take far too long to break down from an environmental point of view. And it's said that the dog poop in landfill has a direct effect on the amount of methane gas coming out of these sites. So surely there is a more environmentally friendly way of dealing with this problem.

Dogs' business at home

First things first – buy yourself a poop scoop! I have a coal shovel that I use to retrieve all the morning parcels in the garden. With four dogs, I am probably what is considered an environmentalist's nightmare, the one saving grace being that mine are mini dogs . . . with mini stools.

There are a few options you have in dealing with your

poop mountain at home. The first is to compost it, but a giant steaming pile of s**t in the corner of your garden may not suit you. And you cannot mix the poop in with your normal compost heap as it will contaminate it. (Dog faeces contains certain pathogens that can be dangerous and shouldn't be used in a garden to fertilise food crops or where children may play.)

So what about flushing it? Flushing, as we know, uses water, and some local authorities aren't equipped to treat the pathogens in the poop that goes into our water system once flushed down the loo. Imagine if everyone started flushing all their dogs' 'business' – I'd definitely turn to bottled water!

So what about making a hole in a corner of your garden to bury it? Well, I don't think that's sustainable because, eventually, your garden will be pitted with small holes of unspeakables. I also learned that over time, if it's near a watershed, the excrement can leak pathogens into our ground water and, ultimately, get into our rivers and seas.

Then there are specifically designed dog composting bins. You can bury them and they do the composting for you with a little water added. And, because they are sealed units, you won't get the floating stink in the air from decomposing poo. But it will still drain into the water table, which is something we should be seriously considering.

The last and probably the best solution I've come up with is a dog-poo wormery. And if you can get past the fact that the worms in question have an unspeakable job breaking down this matter and it won't keep you awake at night, it does seem like a good option. You can then dig the composted poop into your flower beds and borders (just never where children play or where edible foods or fruit trees grow).

When the children are older and no longer interested in helping me plant out flowers and dig in the garden, this is something I will definitely consider; but for now, I'm stuck with choosing the least of all evils. Quality biodegradable bags? Or a compost that goes into the ground?

To be clear, though, while we all have a duty to reduce the volume of plastics that goes into our landfill, this is not a reason to not pick up after your dog. Dog waste is absolutely awful – it stinks, it's grim, it carries diseases and there can't be a soul in this country who hasn't stood in excrement at some point and had their day tainted by it.

So think carefully and choose whatever is right for your circumstances and your household – but just make sure it's never left behind.

8

FEEDING THE SOUL – GOING THAT MINDFUL EXTRA MILE

Dogs are so much more intelligent and perceptive than we used to think decades ago. And knowing that our behaviour, energy and lifestyles have an effect on our dogs' quality of life, as well as their thoughts and feelings, it stands to reason that things like mindfulness, yoga and meditation can positively impact their mental health, too.

Energy Transfer

As I've already mentioned, energy is everything in the dog world. Ever noticed how your dog is so receptive to one person and not another? How your groomer can brush and trim them without them batting an eyelid; or how your vet can administer vaccinations without eliciting any reaction. Whereas some people or other dogs, who seem friendly enough, just rub your dog up the wrong way? Well, it's all in the energy.

Dogs are such feeders on the energy of those around them, whether two-legged or four-legged – so it's important that we take note and understand how our own energy and that of our home will affect them. A nine-to-five manic environment like a daycare centre, for example, where no time out is offered, isn't a normal state for a dog to be in; maintaining such high levels of energy all the time is not beneficial to them and could result in them starting to display unwanted behaviour.

As a groomer, I often see how dogs mirror parental behaviour: a nervous guardian with their nervous dog, an excitable one with their over-the-top dog and a quiet one with their quiet dog. It's quite astonishing how they mimic our energy levels, and how this becomes a learned behaviour for them.

Energy transfer can be applied to everyday routines and activities to keep your dog calm, confident and feeling happy. If you want a starting point from which to alter your energy and to spend some time practising positive energy transfer with your dog, start with some basic meditative practices. Grab a treat for them and then, armed with a meditation playlist, take yourself and them off to a quiet room:

🐾 Sitting on the floor, start with your breathing. Paying attention to your breaths in and out, slow them down, finding some calm. Your dog may be diddling around at this point, standing, looking at you, wondering what planet you are on, but give it time.

🐾 Encourage fuzz head to lie down with you. Reward them, keep their focus and start by very slowly increasing the frequency of the rewards: for them to just be there with you, then to be quiet, reward again. You may hear them give out a big huff and a sigh; that's great – reward! (That is their way of expelling energy and calming down.)

Practise this every week, for ten minutes or half an hour – let the dog decide how long (they will get up and leave, letting you know they've had enough). It's a fabulous bonding activity and you will both feel a million dollars afterwards.

Calm and Present

Here I am banging on about being calm again! Calm is essential – not just for our dogs but for us, too. Calm dogs can lower our blood pressure, help us to release endorphins and offer us some respite from our hectic lives. So let them!

Taking a moment of calm with your dog, whether listening to some relaxing music on your sofa or sitting on a bench somewhere quiet, observing nature is food for your soul. Try to set aside time every day to be present with your pooch for the sake of your own mental wellbeing and theirs.

Whenever you bring awareness to what you're directly experiencing via your senses, or to your state of mind via your thoughts and emotions, you're being mindful. And there's growing research showing that when you train your brain to be mindful, you're remodelling its physical structure.

I've heard that dogs live in the present at all times, but I don't believe that's so. Dogs can be affected by past events and feel insecure about their future, too. We see it in rescue dogs a lot, living off their heightened senses because who knows when their next meal will be. This is something they would worry about through learned behaviour and damage caused by past experiences of abuse, perhaps, or fighting.

To teach our dogs to be in the moment a lot of trust training and confidence building might need to happen first. Being present or living mindfully is about focusing on the here and now, not being distracted by yesterday or tomorrow, nor by negative thoughts and emotions. It's about trying to clear that inner dialogue and find some quiet peace. It's meant to sharpen your focus, too, so if you are feeling you need some help trying to concentrate on a task or an idea, taking time to practise being present is a great skill.

Putting it into action

First, catch your thoughts. How does thinking about tomorrow make you feel? How does thinking about last week make you feel? How do these thoughts in general make you feel?

Now close your eyes, take some deep breaths and then open your eyes again. Notice your surroundings. What are the walls like, what does your dog look like? What can you hear? This is being present in the moment. It focuses you. And it can have transformative effects on you and those around you.

A Peaceful Space

A lot of us, myself included, can be glued to our mobiles, often ignoring our dogs. As I said earlier, both my husband and I are self-employed, so work doesn't stop at five o'clock. It can creep into family time, walks with fuzz heads, dinner time and in the evening, when we are meant to be winding down for the night. We aren't very disciplined, so we have to put a limit on screen time, so we can be present for our dogs and children. Hence, I have implemented no-phone Sundays – a whole day when we are present, spending time with our family and friends (both two- and four-legged), out walking and enjoying the day without distractions.

Social media is wonderful at connecting people, but it can often be a tool via which you start to compare yourself and your level of happiness with others'. It's unrealistic and it can make you feel a little blue. That's not a good mood for our dogs to be around. Why not try an experiment: ditch the socials for a week, or even just a day, and see if you feel better and more present afterwards.

Reiki for Your Pets

I am a reiki practitioner, but I don't practise on other people. I use this therapy as an aid to help me sleep and relax, as that used to be a real issue for me. And I use it on my dogs.

Reiki is a Japanese technique and is all about energy, based on the belief that it flows all through us and that, by using gentle hands above the body, we can help and guide it to heal and relax. Reiki can be used to heal things on so many levels – mentally, physically, spiritually and emotionally. Whether there is a specific injury or it's purely for relaxation, it's just amazing.

I have found that my dogs are especially receptive to reiki – probably because dogs are such energy feeders. It can be done in just five- or ten-minute sessions or longer, up to around thirty minutes – I just let the dog tell me (if they have had enough, they'll get up and saunter off for a snooze and let the healing reiki energy take effect).

Reiki energy has a mind of its own – it knows where it needs to flow – but we can help to guide it by positioning our hands in different areas.

You may think that taking your dog for a reiki session is excessive but giving them the experience of this practice, and the gift of the healing energy it provides, can be so beneficial for them – and for you, too.

Mindful tip

Reiki and massage are not only for when you roll out your yoga mat or light a candle. When you are bathing your dog, for example, you can think about your energy and guide its flow; and rather than just leaving the conditioner to sit on their coat, you can try working it in with some gentle massage.

Doga

Your body and soul crave balance. If anything throws you off balance, your body will freak out and try to correct itself. Yoga is all about balance, and dog yoga – or doga – is basically yoga mixed with dog cuddles in a stress-free environment.

Yoga not only helps our balance, but also strengthens our core, improves posture, helps our heart health and relaxes us – and in our fast-paced lives, don't we all need some extra relaxation? And our dogs can benefit, too. They will pick up on our energy and sense of calm. Plus, it's a beautiful bonding activity to do together.

Doga isn't a gimmick. Many a sceptical yoga aficionado has tried it and been hooked! You have to allow the dog to lead the session, getting involved as much as they want to be. Don't expect too much the first few times. But they might eventually start copying your stretching poses, lying with you during quiet moments and taking the time to slow down together.

You will need a sense of humour, as they'll probably try to lick your face and play with you, but they will soon understand the energy shift. Unlike when I'm doing an exercise class on Zoom and they are all giddy with excitement, tugging on my trainer laces when I'm trying to do my sit-ups. It's a completely different energy for yoga and they know it.

There may not be a yoga class for dogs in your area (there isn't in mine, here in North Yorkshire), but you can join an online class (the variety available today has to be one of the only positives to come out of the pandemic – see Resources, p. 248) or just conduct your own session in your own time, following an online tutorial. So get your mat out, put some music on, grab your pooch and give it a whirl. Because it's all about connection and doing things together – and these exercises are definitely that (even if your pooch is confused by your downward dog!).

Massage

Who doesn't love a massage? I know I do. And our dogs can enjoy it, too.

Massage for your dog should be very gentle, not deep-tissue. As a general guide, the pressure should be 450g–1kg for a small dog and 1.3–3.6kg for a medium to large breed (to get an idea of what that means, get your bathroom scales out and place your hand on them, feeling the pressure).

As you work, you'll need to remember two different massage techniques:

- 🐾 **Effleurage** – long, sweeping strokes (like purposeful stroking of the dog)

- 🐾 **Petrissage** – a stretching, kneading and squeezing technique

The entire process should take place in a calm and quiet environment (although you can also include some elements of massage when you are bathing them or to de-stress them when they are in an uncomfortable situation, like a vet's waiting room).

Here's what to do:

- 🐾 Go into a quiet room where there is little distraction and remove any other dogs. Do one dog at a time, if you have a houseful.

- 🐾 Lay out a blanket and try to have your dog lying on their side. They may not want to do this at first, however, in which case start in the sitting position or standing stance.

- 🐾 Start with effleurage, from their head, down their body and under their rib cage – this will signal to your dog that it is massage time. Begin at the back of their head and use your index and middle fingers to slowly and gently sweep down the spine and back up again. Avoid the bone, placing just one finger on either side. This technique is really calming, especially for dogs who are afraid of touch or anxious dogs.

- 🐾 By now, your dog should be more relaxed and you can move on to their head. On their face, trace your fingers up their nose, starting from the bottom up between their eyes and repeat, in a slow, flowing movement, just as you would on a baby. Their heads are particularly sensitive, and they seem to love this touch between their eyes. It can be very sleep inducing!

🐾 Now move on to the ears, running your hands down them and giving them a gentle tug at the tips. With flowing movements, you are increasing the blood supply to the area you are working on. On the roots of the ears (where they meet the skull), switch up to some petrissage and very gently knead the base of the ears, moving down to the tips. I also use petrissage on the cheeks, as dogs can hold a lot of tension in their jaws and a muscle massage in this area is super relaxing. Remember to always keep one hand on the dog at all times to maintain the connection.

🐾 Moving on from the face, return to using effleurage strokes over the neck and body, your hands flowing one after the other in a continuous stream of thoughtful strokes, skimming over any joints and remaining aware that pressure shouldn't be applied over these areas. You can use small, circular motions over the dog's muscles. By this point, hopefully, they'll be fully relaxed on their side and enjoying their 'me' time.

🐾 Working down the dog's legs to their feet, use your hands under the pads and on top of their toes to gently stretch the toes out and give them a gentle massage. And all the while you should be giving your dog a thorough MOT: checking between their toes for grass seeds, checking armpits and the normally awkward-to-reach areas and using your hands to feel for any anomalies under the skin and new lumps or scrapes.

🐾 Throughout your session, keep gauging how your dog feels. They may walk off to start with but allow them the freedom to come back or leave, as they wish, especially the first few times. It's all new, and they may feel unsure (rescue dogs in particular may not feel relaxed with this level of handling).

🐾 If your dog has had an accident or injury or if they are older and suffering with their legs, their joints and their mobility, this is where professional input from a canine massage specialist would be advised. But you can still try some gentle basic compression techniques on the oldies; these can be used on their rear legs and the base of their necks, with light circular motions to work over the muscles and avoiding the joints to increase blood supply and promote healing.

Massage is a beautiful bonding exercise and one built on trust. The only downside I can see is that your dog will never return the favour!

Meditation

Often, when we are interacting with our dogs at home, we are whizzing around busily, trying to get ready for the day and ensuring they get their walk. Home can be a noisy and chaotic place, so ensuring some quiet time out is a beautiful reset button. Taking five minutes to meditate with your dog can help you both to relax and lower blood pressure. It's most effective when they have had their walk, as they are settled and fulfilled.

If you wish, play some relaxing meditation music to set the tone. Then, sit on the floor with your dog on a rug or blanket. You know where your dog likes to be petted

– maybe they like an ear rub, a chin tickle or their back softly stroked? Transfer some calm energy to them, using a soothing, quiet voice, ensuring your petting is slow and meaningful. Allow them to get comfortable, encouraging them to sit or lie down if they wish. Start by closing your eyes and slowing down your own breath, breathing in deeply for three seconds, holding that breath for four seconds and exhaling for five seconds. Repeat ten times minimum, as you both relax and feel the change in energy.

These little shifts in energy can also be used to help a hyped-up dog to calm down before leaving the house for a walk. Rather than shooting out the door in a flurry of excitement, take a moment to kneel with them by the door, soothingly stroking them and using the same breathing pattern described above.

Sound Matters

We listen to a lot of music in our house. Although, admittedly, sometimes there is a clash in taste (Disney songs on repeat can grow a little tiresome and I'm not always in the mood for my husband's house music when I'm worn out).

Music has a huge effect on how we feel. Imagine it's a sunny day, you're in the car and stuck in a traffic jam, but there are some great tunes on the radio – somehow it's not so bad, is it? Conversely, a sad song on a TV programme can soon get the tears rolling. Well, dogs respond to music, too.

I remember reading a study many years ago in which the stress and anxiety levels of several dogs were monitored while they listened to different genres of music.[2] Pop music

---

2 https://emerginginvestigators.org/articles/music-s-effect-on-dogs-heart-rates/pdf

made them excitable, classical relaxed them and heavy rock – well, that stressed them out (with the exception of one dog who grew up in a household that always listened to heavy rock, so had become desensitised to it).

When the fireworks start on Bonfire Night in the UK and New Year's Eve, too, a popular classical-music radio station has a show dedicated to relaxing dogs (and other pets). The ebb and flow of the melodic music is very calming.

So whenever we think about the behaviour we would like to see in our dogs, we need to consider their environment, too. What are they listening to? It's pretty hard to relax in my house with 'Baby Shark' on repeat and everyone jumping around, I know that. But there are many relaxing playlists available to download and stream, or even just the radio. Dogs can't read or watch television so, when you go out, put on a playlist for them.

Being Mindful in Nature

As far as I'm concerned, there is nothing more uplifting than getting out and about with my dogs. It truly is food for the soul. If I am ever having a down day, it's so lovely to pack a flask, some water and a snack and to take myself and my dogs into the countryside. It has such restorative effects.

Today, for example, I went to Nidderdale (my local countryside) and found the most gorgeous wood. It was carpeted with bluebells and wild garlic, the trees were just out in leaf and the birds were busying themselves with their springtime activities. The wood was strewn with mossy logs, surrounded by ferns, and I just sat for half an hour, basking in the dappled spring sunshine, letting my dogs be dogs, rooting though the forest bed and sniffing all the sniffs. They were so happy, every now and again looking around to check I was still on my chosen rock. I allowed them the freedom to romp around the wood and I enjoyed the peace, too – not on my phone, being still and listening to the sounds of the countryside. I looked at everything, appreciated everything. It was honestly rejuvenating.

Even on a wet day, as long as you are all togged up correctly, the woods can be a glorious place to explore and a haven for our pals. I think woodland walks are my favourite.

So cherish your walks with your friend and remember – it doesn't have to be a constant fast-moving frog march. Take a moment to just sit, too. Sitting gives your dogs a chance to explore further and to feel free to be dogs. That's soul food.

9

HANDLING IN A POSITIVE WAY

It's vital that the connection between you and your dog is an invincible bond of strength and trust.

Our dogs look to us so much for how to feel, think and be, and trust is a massive thing. You can train a dog without it, but then it's usually a relationship based on fear and oppression. That is never the way to go and will not lead to a true bond or connection.

As previously mentioned, each and every dog is unique, and this is something that should be reflected in your handling. As a groomer, yes, I do fancy haircuts, but at least 50 per cent of what I do is reading a dog's body language and slightly altering my handling to suit each one. And this applies to every dog, in every situation.

When to Start

Handling should be started early, when you first collect your little pup. Of course, this isn't always possible if you get a rehomed or a rescue dog, but start as soon as you can. It will make your life easier down the line if you put in the legwork now getting them used to it.

Start slowly, using cues like 'Teeth,' then looking in their mouth and rewarding; or say 'Paws,' then checking between their toes; 'Ears,' then look in their ears. Through your verbal cues, the dog becomes aware of what you are doing. I just start by having a look, and then praise, 'Yes!' and reward, giving them a titbit.

If you have a medium or small dog, get yourself a non-slip mat (like a yoga mat, for example) and pop it on a surface with your dog on top. Use a collar and ask someone to help handle them to start with, so there isn't chaos with the woofer trying to run away, and you're not trying to train a distracted dog. Begin with short bursts – literally one minute to start with – and keep things super calm and positive.

Aim to handle areas we don't often touch, such as their armpits or tail, but pair this with something really positive, like their lick mat (a flat mat made of a rubber material and covered in bristles and ridges, designed to be licked continuously) covered in their favourite treat. This association will map out touch as something positive and enjoyable and not something to avoid.

The goal with handling is that your dog gets used to being touched in this way, so that if you ever need to administer, say, ear drops for an ear infection, remove some contraband from their mouth or check their paws for grass seeds, it's not an impossible task. Plus, your vet and your groomer will really thank you for it.

Handling Different Personalities

With a nervous dog, your energy and body language need to be coaxing and encouraging. With a confident dog, you will be trying to calm them down. (My excitable greeters frantically leap and lunge with licks in a haven't-seen-you-in-ages sort of way!) With an aggressive dog, you want to bring a super-calm, non-threatening energy, as you wouldn't want to trigger them.

As you are probably aware, you need to be very careful handling an aggressive dog and make sure that they are safe and aren't going to hurt you, anyone else or themselves. I've met a few people whose dogs have turned on them now and again and they really are nervous handling them, visibly jumping, both parties looking at each other with nervous flicks of the eyeballs. We want our dogs to be relaxed and happy sausages, and that means having a calm and confident handler. With this in mind, there is nothing wrong with muzzling a dog for safety, and I have found that once a muzzle is secured, they accept it and the energy changes completely.

Greetings

On meeting any dog, I would allow them to approach me. I don't make eye contact, I am calm and never pushy and I will get down to their level and turn to the side.

After the initial interactions, if I need to handle the dog for my job, I pop them on my table and spend time quietly talking to them encouragingly. My movements are always predictable and gentle, reassuring them, gently and slowly stroking them and constantly watching their body language – are they tense? Are they relaxed?

I always keep one hand on the dog at all times. They feel that I am confident, and this gives them that connection. In turn, this means that I can feel those first muscle movements when they want to get away or if they are particularly tense and uneasy, and offer a reassuring touch.

I know my craft and that confident and gentle handling is really reassuring to the dog. Take nail trimming, for instance: I am fast and safe with clipping a dog's nails and, if they are a regular, they trust me and it's all done in a second. If, however, you are inexperienced with nail trimming, it's more than likely the dog will resist somewhat. They are master readers and will sense your unease with the task straight away. Then they will feel uneasy themselves. So being confident really does pay off.

So many of my customers say they cannot believe I can groom their dogs, brush them or even bathe them so easily, as they have to chase them out from behind the sofa, catch them and then wrestle them into the bath. Then they have a wet dog on the loose, rampaging around the house. And they can't even think about getting that brush and hair dryer out. It sounds hilarious, but it can be stressful. Here again – your energy, your body language, tone of voice and attitude are everything.

Distractions Can Be Your Friend

If you are trying to brush a fluffy who doesn't like it or who is in training, use something like a lick mat to distract them and also have their favourite toy or a high-value treat on hand to create a positive association with the experience. But with some very nervous dogs, you will find they may not want any treats at all and aren't in a relaxed enough state to feel comfortable eating, so small bursts are best for them: first, let them look at the brush, just being in its presence, then reward (with praise, attention, a toy or treat) and work up from there. Again, it's all about positive associations and, with repetition, it becomes a learned behaviour. (We will discuss grooming in more detail in Chapter 10).

That Reassuring Hand

It's a myth that you can't reassure a nervous or anxious dog. People used to think that by reassuring them you were reinforcing their nervous anxiety, but that's not true. Dogs do respond positively to reassurance and it makes them feel safe.

Never, ever punish a dog for being nervous or anxious. It will only make it worse and make them fearful of you – not to mention it's just not right. With nervous behaviour, accept that you are in it for the long haul, that nothing will be fixed in one session and that it's often something you will have to manage over a long period, slowly and steadily counter-conditioning with baby steps.

Say you have guests coming round and your dog is nervous with strangers. Allow them to have an escape route if things get difficult – to be able to take themselves into their crate if that's their quiet place, or out of the way, upstairs. Politely explain to your guests that he/she has stranger danger, they won't want to be petted and that they should please ignore them. This is important – I find with my nervous girl that there is always that one person who thinks they are Dr Dolittle (the dog whisperer, the one who can change the dog's ways) and they will do the whole coochie-coochie thing with their fingers and stare at her.

As an aside, not all dogs want to be petted. One of mine only likes me, my husband and close members of the family to pet her. She can even be uncomfortable when my children pet her – never nasty, but she will lick her lips (a sign of anxiety) and walk away. My children, although both under five, respect this. I have been really strict with them where this is concerned, as it's super important and something I feel very strongly about. Only last week, we were in town and I saw a woman sitting on a bench watching her small child fuss over a dog who I could see wasn't into it at all.

This can be so dangerous.

Back to the handling, though. Whatever the cause of the anxiety, the handling needs to be patient and calm and you have to offer them security and reassurance. Don't push them too much; dogs can become easily overwhelmed.

Note: while you can help your dog with low-level anxiety, if it's a more serious issue I would recommend you seek professional help – you will see positive results much more quickly that way.

Mindful tip

Dogs are fantastic mindfulness teachers. They don't have cluttered minds like we do and can focus on what is in front of them. So why not try taking a little time out every day to practise mindfulness with your dog, even for just a couple of minutes, to clear your mind?

Stroke your dog, concentrating purely on the sensation of touch. How does their fur feel? How do their ears feel? Envelop them in a cuddle (as long as they're willing) – what do they smell like? (My dogs' feet smell like popcorn!) Then think about the emotions you are feeling in that moment.

Things That Can Help

During stressful times like a house move, firework displays or whatever else triggers your dog, there are various products you can try that will help to calm and relax them, getting them through trickier periods in their life.

I first tried a dog wrap for a TV show I was doing and the feedback from users was fantastic. You can buy branded wraps or there are videos online showing you how to make your own, but the principle behind them is that they're a bit like a hug or a swaddle. The pressure of the wrap can release oxytocin and endorphins to make the dog feel calmer. Here are some other things that can be helpful:

- **Dog-appeasing pheromone collars and home plug-ins** These synthetically mimic the natural pheromones in dogs to help anxiety.

- **Calming sprays** These contain a unique blend of essential oils, like lavender and rose.

- **Calming treats** These contain things like valerian root, hemp oil and camomile – all of which are known to be calming.

- **CBD oil** This isn't just beneficial for humans but for dogs, too, and dog-specific versions can be added to their food.

- **Valerian compound** This is a natural remedy that helps to relax the pathways within the nervous system. Again, this should be a dog-specific product.

And, of course, there is always massage, which can work wonders – for full instructions on carrying out a canine massage, see p. 155.

Understanding the Mechanics of Our Dogs

A dog's joints are like ours – ball-and-socket and lever joints. Their front legs are levers where they join the body, and their back legs are ball-and-socket. With this in mind, care should be taken when handling, whether that's putting on their harness or towelling off a mud monster after a wet-weather walk. Think of your own knees – they only go forwards and backwards, never sideways.

Dogs' feet contain many bones and whether you are a professional trimming their nails or you just want to wipe their paws, you have to handle them correctly – gently. I pick up my dogs' paws at the pastern (the area of their leg below their wrist or heel and above their foot); I then cup the foot with my hand, placing my thumb behind the main paw pad, leaving the foot free and open for inspection. I don't squeeze or apply too much pressure.

If you need to handle muddy paws but your dog keeps snatching them away, don't let go, but don't squeeze harder either – that's only going to cause them discomfort. Instead, go with them, following into their body, then gently encourage the leg back out again to clean. If they are adamant, I find that a change in body position can help. Try asking the dog to stand and then bring the front foot under their body. Sometimes having them in a different position entirely and inspecting their feet from under them can change their behaviour. But be aware that older dogs may be suffering with arthritis and their feet may genuinely be painful to touch. So watch out for those behavioural changes (see p. 235).

If they are used to your touch, but still resistant, think about *how* you are handling. Is it comfortable for them? Are you projecting the right energy (calm and confident)? Can you alter your body position to a more favourable one for them? Could you offer them a distraction like a lick mat? Have you worked on touch with them? If not, start a plan for counter-conditioning them, with small bursts of training and their favourite food or reward. Eventually, they will look forward to that training time and handling won't be something they dread, worry about or shy away from.

Handling When Out Walking

We'd all like a dog that doesn't pull right, walks effortlessly and serenely beside us and sits at every kerb. What a dream! But in reality, loose-lead walking is the hardest thing to teach your dog, so, if you have a zigzagger, a sled dog in a Dalmatian's body or a plodder who enjoys the view of your rear end, I can guarantee you are not alone. (I have found some of my dogs much easier to train to walk with a loose lead than others. I find the males harder – maybe because they have their coconuts and think with them half the time!)

The principle behind training your pal to walk with a loose lead the kind way – the way that would make your dog the happiest and most trusting of you – is that when they are pulling nothing happens. You don't check them, you don't tell them off. All they experience is resistance on the lead. But when they check in with you when walking with a loose lead, wonderful things happen and hotdogs rain from the sky! After some time, they think: Well, if I pull nothing happens, but if I check in with the lead bearer and stop pulling, good things happen. This method of training does take longer than some of the more traditional ones, but it's a method built on trust, love and the most fantastic bond.

PACK-LEADER THEORY DEBUNKED

Handling and raising a dog involves many different approaches and styles. Some people still talk
about the guardian being the pack leader and that
you have to be a dominant, alpha, boss-like figure,
demanding respect and obedience. This way of
handling and training can get pretty fast results, but it
doesn't cure any issue a dog may have, like aggression, nuisance barking or maybe pulling on a lead.
Rather, assertive, dominance-type handling and training simply worries your dog into submission and results
in them burying their emotions.

Even wolves in the wild don't have a pack leader.
Everything is done for the good of the pack – their family
group – and they all work together. So the pack-leader
theory, whereby we assert ourselves as our dogs' alpha, is
nonsense. Dogs aren't like humans fighting for hierarchy
and status; they simply don't understand this concept.

Give your dog some credit and the respect they deserve
– they know you're not a dog in their pack; they're well
aware that you are a two-legged alien/human being. If you
have a bossy or seemingly dominant dog, it's likely that
they feel insecure or anxious, and being dominant or heavy-
handed when handling them will only damage their trust
and confidence.

Instead, you should model calm leadership and gently
guide them using your reassuring touch, relaxed energy and
positive associations.

Whether your dog is a puppy, an adult or an oldie, your handling needs to be consistent, calm and kind. We know how much dogs rely on us for their happiness and how big a part trust plays in their lives, so, armed with this knowledge and all the skills you have learned in every aspect of canine care, you can become the most amazing, in tune and considerate handler for your dog.

10

GROOMING MARVELLOUS

This isn't a grooming guide (although I should write one!). But some space should nevertheless be devoted to something your dog will have to go through their whole life. After all, whether they're the marshmallow-resembling Bichon or the short-haired doting Labrador, they all need some element of grooming, and this is my *Mastermind* specialist subject.

Building a Relationship

Dog grooming is an unregulated industry, with new groomers, seasoned groomers, some with qualifications and some without. So finding the right professional is important, and I do believe that once you find one you are happy with, you should stick with them and build a relationship. Then they, in turn, will gain an understanding of your dog's history, their quirks, their likes and dislikes.

Not all dogs enjoy the grooming process, so it is important that a relationship based on trust is established. We tend to think of it as a bit of a spa day, but the reality for your dog is that there's a lot of handling involved, which they may not be used to, a bath, which some don't enjoy so much, as well as noise in the salon, which can be difficult for them to deal with.

Your dog has a lifetime of handling, brushing and bathing ahead of them. And even if you have a short-coated dog who may not need grooming in the sense of haircuts, etc.,

THE WASHING MYTH

One grooming myth I'd like to dispel is that dogs can't be washed regularly because it strips their coats of natural oils.

Well, going back thirty years or so, 'dog shampoo' as we know it now wasn't available on the mass market. Instead, we made our dogs stand outside and pointed the cold hose at them, then slathered them in washing-up liquid. Horrendous! (Maybe that's why dogs seem to be predisposed to love river swimming but hate bath time?) The washing-up liquid would dry out a dog's coat and skin and the cold water wasn't good for the joints, especially for older dogs. Even human shampoo is not good, as dogs have a completely different pH level to us. So we need to use a specific quality dog shampoo that matches their pH level. I try go for one that is natural and sulfate- and phosphate-free. A good-quality shampoo followed by a good-quality conditioner enhances both coat and skin.

I bathe my dogs every week (they have long coats, so it's necessary to keep them in optimum condition). And it's fine to wash your dog frequently at home (I wash my show dogs every three to four days), as long as you follow the guidance in this chapter.

they will still be absolutely lifting the roof off your house after a month without a bath – so they, too, should have a positive introduction to the grooming process, if only from a hygiene perspective.

When to Start

I don't know who introduced the idea that a dog shouldn't be groomed until they are six months old, but it's completely wrong. In fact, when dogs are young, that is exactly the time to start gradually introducing them to new things: the bath, the noise of a hair dryer, the sound of clippers (not applicable to smooth/ very short-coated breeds) and being handled by a stranger (who, as mentioned, you should stick with, as chopping and changing professional groomers isn't good for the dog).

I start grooming my own dogs as soon as possible. Once your puppy has had all their vaccinations (see p. 45), take them to a groomer for their first bath, blow-dry and nail trim. Then, two weeks to a month later, they should go back for another bath, blow-dry and also to clear their eyes (if their breed requires this), have a nail trim, clear the hair off their privates and tidy around their toes. Then I would build up from there, so that by four months they will have experienced a full haircut, even if it's just a light tidy all over, and will start to understand the process and the groomer's routine.

Equipment

Equipment we may use at home and in the salon for the dog needs to be introduced early and will include the following:

- 🐾 A hair dryer
- 🐾 A shower head
- 🐾 Clippers
- 🐾 Vacuum cleaner
- 🐾 A toothbrush

I mention the vacuum cleaner because it's a great tool to use for noise-desensitisation practice. It's something we all have at home and it makes a similar noise to that of the blaster dryers or high-velocity dryers used in grooming salons. You don't want a dog that spins into a stupor every time you try to give them a blow-dry, nor do you want them attacking the vacuum cleaner at home, whether in play or fear. You want them to be comfortable around everything in the home and the grooming salon.

With anything noisy like the vacuum or the hair dryer, introduce them to it slowly at home. I start by just having pooch in the same room as the machine, switched off. Scatter treats around it and let them investigate and smell it. Once they are comfortable in the presence of the machine, get a lick mat or a treat toy with their favourite spread or treats in and turn the machine on with them at a distance. Don't do anything else. If they react and aren't comfortable with the noise, calmly switch it off and take it into the next room, leaving them with their treat. Then turn it on in the other room, starting further away. Repeat as necessary, until you get to a point where they don't react to the noise, want to run a mile or assume attack mode. Build up using the same technique, until you start moving the machine around a little. Start in short bursts and keep your actions slow and controlled. With a vacuum, I show them a mat they can lie on with their treat, so they have a base and you can work around them.

Once desensitisation has worked, you can move on to the hair dryer. Pop a yoga mat on a table for small or medium dogs or on the floor for bigger dogs and ask someone to help you engage the dog and reward them. Move the dryer closer and start blow-drying their rear first (furthest away from their heads). If the dog shows interest, that's fine, but, if they react badly to having the dryer near them but not turned on, go back a few steps and keep practising. If you have other dogs in the house who are used to the noise, they really can learn from their friends, so get another dog on the table and give them a blow-dry instead. I find in my salon that the youngsters really do learn from watching others.

The same technique can be used for introducing any new tools and sounds involved in performing a groom.

Grooming Relationships

Whether you are building a grooming relationship with your own dog or as a professional groomer with someone else's, it should be a bonding activity. I talk calmly to the dogs in my care, and if they are a little worried (wide-eyed, trembling, very stiff, whining or panting), I reassure them. They live with humans, so most will respond to a soothing voice.

I think of every groom, every brushing session as being about building trust. That's why everything – from the way we handle the dog and respond to their cues to how we go about brushing out knots – is important. If you are too rough, too heavy-handed or you are trying to control the dog too much, they will lose trust in you.

I'm a safe groomer. I know my way around my tools and how to handle them all in such a way as to complete a groom without any drama or trauma. My confidence around my tools and equipment, my handling techniques and my belief in my own ability to read a dog's body language make a dog feel at ease, knowing they are in safe hands.

Confidence is important – so if in doubt, fake it until you make it. So many dog guardians are astounded when they watch me groom – seeing their dogs are so compliant with the process, willingly letting me trim out their pads and offering up their legs for a brush out. They always comment that they can't get anywhere near them at home, and it becomes a game of Tom and Jerry, with them wielding the brush while their pup darts behind the sofa in search of sanctuary.

So be conscious of your own body language: in anything you do – be it washing, brushing or drying – say to yourself, 'I've got this. I know what I am doing. Everything is just swell.'

Bathing – Down to Business

Right – you are now ready to bathe your dog at home. You are feeling confident, you know what products to use and you have chosen the right spot (your own bath or a large shower).

Get yourself organised – the last thing you want is to be searching for a suitable towel while your pal makes a bid for the carpet for a darned good roll around! I keep a duffle bag ready for action, containing my home-bathing kit:

- A plastic 2-litre measuring jug

- A bath scrunchie/shower puff

- Dog-specific shampoo and conditioner

- Cotton wool (just a blob for inside each ear to protect them when rinsing)

🐾 Non-slip bath mat (you know, the rubber ones with suckers on the underside)

🐾 A super-absorbent faux chamois leather (honestly, this is a game changer – if there's any moisture, these guys find it and suck it out of the coat, plus it really helps speed up your drying time)

🐾 Two towels (one for the floor and one to go around the dog)

🐾 And, if you have a leaper (a dog who hangs its whole self as far out of the bath as is possible, drenching your floors), get an industrial sucker with a ring on it; this sticks to the side of the bath and you can attach it to a grooming lead or bath loop (this is not with a view to retraining the dog, but just to save your bathroom floors and stop that urge to leap out and make a run for it)

Next, follow these steps for a trauma-free experience:

🐾 Mix a solution of shampoo in the plastic measuring jug. Generally, this will be around one part shampoo to twenty parts water, but check the directions on the label of your shampoo, as it can vary (and some should be used neat).

🐾 Apply the bubbly mixture to your dog's coat with your bath scrunchie and hands (no need to pre-wet your pal). Start on their back, working methodically all over their body, being sure not to miss anywhere – their bottom, especially! – and wash down their legs to their feet. You will also be mapping your dog with your hands – are they overweight, underweight or just right? Can you feel any strange lumps or bumps or new grazes to keep an eye on? This is your time to give them an MOT with your fingertips. And you can check their skin condition when you blow-dry.

🐾 After the dog's whole body has been washed, move on to their head. Make sure you have put a blob of cotton wool in each ear – just the part you see when you look inside, never down the ear canal. Tell them how clever and wonderful they are and then wash their face, paying attention to ear leathers and chins. I use my fingers and thumbs to gently rub the solution in over the face, avoiding their eyes. If you do get some in their eyes, just rinse with water straight away.

🐾 Once the face is shampooed, it's time to rinse off the whole dog. Start on the head and elevate the nose, so the water doesn't go down their snout (this is very important), and clasp the top of the ear canal to stop the water entering their ears, too. Rinse their chin and then move on to their back. There is no point rinsing their legs before this, as the shampoo on their backs will run on to their already rinsed legs.

🐾 I remove excess water from the coat using the faux chamois like a towel. (Don't rub medium-to-longer coats as this will create knots – instead, just squeeze.)

🐾 Now it's time for their conditioner, for optimum shine, softness and to replenish the coat. Again, you should read the product's instructions, but I do like to make a cream rinse with my conditioner, rather than apply it neat. This not only helps your product to go further, but I find it also helps it to cover and soak into the whole coat.

🐾 The next step is to give your dog a relaxing massage (see p. 155). This helps to stimulate blood supply (and the oxygenated blood has rejuvenating properties), it's relaxing and enjoyable for the dog and it gives the conditioner time to work into the coat (like our own hair conditioner, it's more effective if left on for ten minutes).

🐾 Time for that final rinse. Watch out for shaking, or you may end up looking like you've taken part in a wet T-shirt competition! On some dogs, just placing your hands over their withers/shoulders stops their urge to shake, but this doesn't work on all dogs. (I remember a German Shepherd I used to groom that would shake the water off throughout the bathing process – I'm not sure which of us was wetter by the end.) So be prepared that your bathroom might resemble a water park by the time you've finished, although hopefully it will be more like a calm spa with a clean dog at the end.

Practice definitely makes perfect with bathing but, if it is just too big a job to tackle in your bathroom at home, book your dog in for their regular bath with your friendly local grooming expert. They are prepared for and don't mind all the shenanigans.

You might sometimes need to do a hose-off outside following a muddy walk, so speak to your plumber about installing a hot-water feed outside your home. The warmer water will be much kinder to your dog's limbs and they will be far happier being hosed off this way – and that's so important, especially as you do not to want to instil a water fear or reluctance in them.

Brushing Up

Brushing your dog and getting them dried after the bath entirely depends on their coat type.

🐾 **Smooth coats** This refers to short, close-cropped hair that is very fine and somehow weaves into every item of clothing. Breed examples include Weimaraner, Dalmation, Boxer and Smooth-coated Dachshund. These coats are nice and easy to dry – you just chamois off as much as possible; for bigger dogs you place a towel over your legs and encourage them to lie with you, while for smaller dogs you put a yoga mat on a table with a towel on top, which will really save your back! (No point having a beautified dog if you are bent double and unable to appreciate that beauty.) Use your hair dryer on low to start with and, using a rubber brush, gently brush where you are drying, starting farthest away from the head and being extra gentle over joints. Be careful not to overbrush or to brush too hard. The rubber helps to remove any loose hair ,which your home will be thankful for (and your dinners, too – we joke that we rarely ate a meal without finding a Dobermann hair in it).

🐾 **Short coat** This is short hair but with a thick undercoat – a great waterproof coat and thicker than you would maybe initially imagine. Breed examples include Labrador, Rottweiler and Pug – these guys love to moult. The technique here is similar to drying smooth coats, but you can also use a de-shedding tool, designed to remove the undercoat and loose hair without cutting or damaging the topcoat. Be gentle here, and, if you are in any doubt, visit your professional groomer for a de-shedding treatment.

Wire coat This is wiry to the touch and typically seen in Terriers (scruffy little blighters that they are) – Border Terriers, Lakeland Terriers and Welsh Terriers. I dry these dogs using a palm pad or a soft slicker brush, moving the coat while using the hair dryer to help dry the coat in the direction of growth, taming their locks to lie as flat as possible. You can use a moult brush to remove dead hair growth, too, but be careful not to remove too much undercoat, especially if they are hand stripped. (Hand stripping is a very old technique used for some wire- and silky-coated breeds, whereby the 'blown' or loose topcoat is pulled out by hand; it isn't painful and leaves space in the dog's hair follicle for fresh, new growth.) The wire coat can be very deceptive; you might think it's dry but, two minutes later, it's damp again. You need to make sure the whole coat is dry, so use your fingertips to delve in and see if you can feel any damp (if so, more drying is needed).

Wool and combination coats I've put these two coat types together – the woolly clouds of fluff and the velvet teddies of the dog world – because I dry them in much the same way. Wool breed examples include Poodles, Bichons, and Bedlington Terriers. Examples of the combination coat are cross breeds like the Cockapoo, Cavapoo and the Schnoodle, although, as they are a mix, they can resemble one or other of their parentage more (either more woolly or more silky). Once they are settled and ready for drying, I use my hair dryer to create a rosette in the hair – a parting if you will – and then, using a soft slicker brush, I brush wherever the air flow from the dryer is, working methodically through the hair, paying special attention to the ears, legs, armpits and tail (any longer areas of hair). This method of stretch drying, where we use brushing along with the hair dryer to dry the coat straight, also helps to ensure that it's knot free. Some people do prefer the curly, natural look, but these guys can't be left to dry naturally; it will only create coat issues for you and, as their coats are one of their best assets (along with those eyes and that waggy tail), taking proper care of them is important. If you want the curls, just dampen the hair down after a thorough blow-dry and they will return.

Don't be scared of the slicker brush – you are brushing the hair and not the skin, and you should be gentle enough to get through the hair but not irritate the skin from overbrushing one area (something we call slicker burn). Once the coat is dry, I use a metal comb to run through it, checking for any knots and tangles. If you do find any, remove the comb and go back to your brush. (For more on tangle, see p. 189.)

Long, silky coats These are the coat models of the dog world. They could be something off a L'Oreal advert; with their flowing barnets and stunning silhouettes, these coats are like strands of gold and need to be treated with the utmost respect. Breed examples include the Afghan Hound, Full-coated Lhasa, Shih Tzu and Yorkshire Terrier. You have to be careful drying this coat not to let the air flow from your dryer whip it up into knots. Point the dryer further away and, using a pin brush, dry the coat in the direction of growth. (We use a pin brush on any longer coat to protect it, to prevent breakage as far as possible.) You may need to use a soft slicker on their legs if the hair is shorter in this area and you are finding you can't brush right down to the skin.

Double coat These are the winter jackets of the dog world – the walking puffer jackets. Designed to withstand cold temperatures, they are waterproof and provide protection from the elements. Breed examples include St Bernards, Siberian Huskies and Rough Collies (or Lassie dogs, if you were born pre-1990). You have your work cut out with these coats, not only bathing these guys properly and penetrating the whole skin and coat, but also ensuring they are thoroughly rinsed and dried. Special bathing attention needs to be paid to their derrières, which can be super hairy and sometimes stinky, too. If you are keen to maintain these breeds at home alongside using your fabulous talented groomer, I suggest you invest in a high-velocity dryer or a blaster (you can pick these up online from as little as £50 or upwards of £600.) I like to use a variable-speed model with an option to add heat (or not). These powerful dryers really help that loose fur to fly, so it may not be something you want to do in your living room. But wherever you choose to dry these guys, the area will need a complete clean down afterwards because, believe me, that hair will be everywhere! And I mean *everywhere*. I blast the coat through, until it's about 80 per cent dry, then use my normal dryer to finish, along with my slicker brush.

BRUSHING TIP

It's really important to brush the whole coat (not just the top layer or the back of the dog) from the top layer all the way to the root. It needs to be brushed and then combed out to prevent uncomfortable knots and mats.

Pay particular attention to the derrière again, ensuring it's knot free. Once you've finished, their coat should look glossy – like they have had the best bouncy blow-dry on the market.

BLOW-DRYING 101

When you are drying a dog, make sure you always brush wherever the dryer is. You shouldn't keep the dryer on one spot on the coat for too long as it is warm, so keep moving it every five seconds: count to five while brushing and then move the dryer 5cm over and continue. Work in a routine over the coat so you don't miss any areas and continue in this pattern. That means the warm air isn't sitting on one place on the dog for too long, getting too hot, and it also means you are working methodically and ensuring the whole coat is dry.

You will have given your dog a thorough hands-on health check in the bath but, now, while you are drying them, you should also be giving them a visual one. Give their skin a really thorough check, looking out for warts (be careful not to brush these, as they have a sensitive blood supply), fleas and ticks and also taking in their overall health: is it scurfy and dry? Or is there a bad oil build-up? What do the feet look like? Check between toes, check their bits and bobs (balls and willy or vagina) are healthy, too, and look for funny discharge, like mucus or blood (other than when your dog is in season, when a female has a swollen vulva and bleeds – this occurs typically every six months). And if there is anything you are unhappy about, speak to your vet.

🐾 **Silky coat** These are a combination of long, silky hair and naturally short areas, too – beautiful to watch when they are moving, like a silk scarf draped over a dog's torso. Breed examples include English Cocker Spaniels, Red Setters and English Springer Spaniels. I like to dry these coats in the direction of hair growth to let that closer hair on their bodies dry as flat as possible and the feathers and furnishings – the longer hair from their tummy, legs and ears – flow off the dog. I use a combination of my slicker brush to move the hair so it dries correctly, and a pin brush and slicker on the legs. I sometimes use a boar-bristle brush, too, as it's softer, so prevents damage, and it helps to smooth the coat and make it beautiful and glossy. Pay close attention to armpits and the backs of their ears – what I call high-friction areas – as the hair is softer there because their ears and legs are moving back and forth constantly, creating this soft hair to easily knot up.

🐾 **Hairless dogs** You may laugh, but these chaps need a bath, too, as they can get really greasy or very dry skin. Breed examples are the Hairless Chinese Crested, American Hairless Terrier and the Mexican Hairless (or Xoloitzcuintli, if you are feeling fancy). A good towel off and gentle blow-dry – never hot – and these guys are good to go (although some have areas of hair that may need drying with a soft brush).

The Importance of Coat Maintenance

So what happens when we don't maintain our dogs' hair correctly? On shorter-haired dogs the coat becomes thick with dead hair, they shed clumps around the house and their skin can't breathe, as it's engulfed in loose hair stuck in their coat.

VISITING THE GROOMER

Visiting places like the groomer or the vet can be daunting for your dog. They smell strange, there are other animals around, strange people, new noises . . . All in all, it can be pretty overwhelming.

If you are sitting with the dog in a waiting room, it's ok to reassure them. As mentioned earlier, the idea that you shouldn't reassure a worried dog because it rewards that behaviour is a fallacy. Just as when we are worried or unsure and a loved one puts their arm around us and reassures us, it's the same for dogs. But don't overdo it. I've seen it taken too far, where the energy of the guardian is hyped up and anxious, too, telling the dog over and over it's ok, furiously patting them, as if they are being sent away to a prison camp. You need to be calm and confident, happy and positive. It's great that your dog is getting a full MOT, so don't worry for them. Rather, they need you to be their rock, so just support them.

Lingering goodbyes are not good in this scenario, cooing at them, walking slowly backwards, popping your head around the door and telling them 'Mummy will only be five minutes'. This doesn't help; it just increases the dog's desire to get to you and makes them realise that their one and only is leaving them. So be kind, positive and reassuring, but don't go too far – just calm and confident enough that your dog will pick up on your vibe.

Not to mention they just don't look their optimum selves. Honestly, when dogs look good, they know it – they have a spring in their step and feel great, so grooming has real benefits for them, too.

On longer coats, the hair becomes tangled. If these tangles are left, they 'make friends' with the nearby hairs and they all join together, creating mats – a big chain gang of knots. These mats spread over the dog's body until, in worst-case scenarios, they are covered from head to toe in one big pelt of hair. This tangled and matted hair is like a straitjacket for the dog, restricting comfortable movement.

Knotted and matted hair also prevents their skin from breathing, reducing circulation. And because air cannot flow through the coat, helping to regulate temperature, they can easily become overheated. Lastly, as if all that isn't enough, it makes your dog completely miserable. So hopefully, you can see how consistently grooming your dog at home and taking them to a professional groomer on a regular schedule is vital to not only their care, but also their happiness.

If you do find some knots, use your brush (slicker brush or pin brush, ideally) to brush the knot on your hand or fingers (not on the dog's skin), then try to tease apart the tangle with your fingers, splitting it in two and brushing again. Then use a comb to check they're all out. Do not use a comb to get knots out, as this will be too painful for the dog.

If you find some mats, don't panic. Just put the brush down and make an appointment with a professional. They can be sorted out by being clipped off short, if necessary. And remember, it's hair – it will grow back. Your dog's happiness and welfare are the most important things here, not their appearance. But with a regular schedule moving forwards with your groomer, they can be in glorious coat.

Nails

A dog's nails are an important part of their anatomy. They feel through their nails and use them to dig and hold on to objects. But they can be a problem if left to get too long. If this happens, they can put pressure on the bones in the toes and cause the feet to change shape; they can also make walking uncomfortable. But dogs are great at masking discomfort, so you may not always notice the signs (of which more below). Too-long nails can also change your dog's gait (how they walk). And in our modern homes, with tiles, wooden floors and slippery surfaces, longer nails will stop them from being able to grip properly with their pads. Nails left to grow can even curl right around the toe and start to grow back into the paw pad. Ouch!

So how do you know if your dog's nails need clipping? Ever heard that tip tap tip tap of nails on your floors? Well, that's a sign that your dog's nails need clipping. Another clue is to stand the dog in front of you and look at their nails on all four feet – are they touching the floor in that standing position? Then get a credit card and see if you can slot it under the nails. If you can't do this, their nails need a clip. The more you clip dogs' nails, especially as puppies, the more the vein (or quick) inside the nail recedes. This is a good thing, as it means the nails can be kept lovely and short, whereas if they are left, the nail grows longer and the vein grows down inside it, and the longer vein makes it impossible to get that nail nice and short again without causing discomfort to the dog. So take your dog to the groomer (or the vet) regularly to have their nails clipped and/or ground down. I would even go so far as to say every fortnight when you first get them, but a good breeder should have been doing them from when the dog was tiny for the comfort of their mother when feeding and to prevent any scratches. Those needle-like nails can even get stuck in bedding and towels, so they should be kept short. With regular trimming, especially from a young age, your dog should not grow very long quicks in the nails.

Plenty of walking should also help to keep nails pretty short but keep a check on them anyway.

Ears

A good way of checking your dog's ear health is to look and smell. Are their ears dirty? Are they bothered by them, scratching and rubbing them? Get your nose in there – is there a bad smell coming from them?

A healthy ear should look much like ours – clean, no redness, no gunk and no smell. Regular cleaning of *just the area you can see* with a cotton pad and some dog-ear cleaner will help to clean general ear wax, but if there are any signs that something is not right, you will need to get your dog checked by your vet for a possible ear infection, ear mites or allergies. Left untreated, ear infections can escalate into a much bigger problem, so routine care and checking is important to keep ears healthy.

Teeth

Just like us, dogs need dental care, especially the smaller breeds.

All dogs have forty-two teeth, whether they are Great Danes or Chihuahuas. (Although with modern breeds dogs have been scaled down in size, their teeth count remains the same.) Our dogs also don't eat the same as their wild ancestors, who spent more time gnawing and chewing on their food; we feed them a lot of soft foods and the treats marketed as 'dental treats' can often have poor nutritional value and are too soft to clean off plaque and tartar build-up (that stuff is like cement on their teeth).

Our pals' gnashers are designed for biting, tearing and chewing on meat, bones and cartilage, so, if they aren't eating like a wild dog, I suggest you toothbrush train them. This will save *you* money in the long run, as dentistry work on your dog is expensive and, more importantly, it will save your dog the discomfort of living with rotting teeth, gum disease and extractions.

Some of the dogs' mouths I've peered into over the years have been horrific sights to behold and, often, people are reluctant to take them for dental treatment, due to the expense and their worries over anaesthetics. Discuss these concerns with your vet, as nowadays there are safer ways of putting a dog under for treatment if they are old. Your dog's oral health is part and parcel of dog husbandry and you have a duty to take proper care of it.

You can use a children's toothbrush or a dog's toothbrush if you fancy. (I don't like those rubber finger brushes; I find a children's or dog's bristle toothbrush better.) You can even get special flavoured toothpastes for dogs (don't use your own because of the amount the dog will ingest; plus, I don't think they enjoy the super-minty fresh taste as much as we do).

I train all my dogs to let me handle their heads and mouths (see p. 163) and, once they are comfortable with this, I introduce the toothbrush. Don't brush too hard, and be aware that there will be a lot of chewing on the tooth-brush at the same time. And pay close attention to the teeth further back, which can be hard to get to.

It might feel like a chore adding things like teeth and ear cleaning for your dog to your already busy week, but it's so much easier if you get yourself organised. I keep my dogs' nail clippers, toothbrushes, toothpaste and the other bits I use regularly for training (like their show leads) together in a cute bag in my kitchen, where it's all easy to access, giving

Mindful tip

When you are giving your dog a brush, you can prac-tise some mindfulness at the same time, enjoying that bonding moment with your dog – just being in the pres-ent and appreciating them and all the love they bring.

You can also use reiki throughout your grooming session and incorporate your new-found massage techniques, too (see p. 155), making the whole process really enjoyable for your dog. I will break off every now and again to look into their eyes, for example, and tell them how clever and wonderful they are.

When you are bathing or grooming your dog, think about your energy, too. Make sure you do it on a day when you are feeling calm and upbeat – remember those micro-movements (see p. 58) and how our dogs are so perceptive of our emotions.

me the eye and reminding me I have to do these things. I also keep a cut-down yoga mat slipped in behind my tea trays, so it's a quick grab when I find five minutes to do my dog-maintenance admin. If this stuff is completely out of sight, it can also be out of mind, and then it's all too easy for a week or two to go by without doing these tasks. It's a bit like my vitamins – I keep them in my fruit bowl, so when I grab a banana in the morning, that's a prompt for me to take them. Or when I go to my dogs' food-bowl cupboard, I'll see the glucosamine supplements, omega oil and meds right there in front of me (see p. 139 for more about these). These things help to make our busy lives easier, by creating habit-forming associations.

11

JOYFUL ACTIVITIES

It's the weekend. At last, you've got some 'you' time – by which I obviously mean you *and* your hairy bestie. But spending time with your dog doesn't have to mean yet another walk in yet another park; their life doesn't have to be all walks and then home to sit on the couch. They get bored, just like we do, walking the same walks all the time, sniffing the same smells from the same passing dogs.

I am a big advocate of hobbies and activities for dogs. Maybe my family background in working dogs (working gun dogs, specifically) instilled in me the idea that dogs like a purpose. But it stands to reason – we do, so why shouldn't our dogs, too? They like something that gets them out for the day; something to look forward to. When I pack my car up for a show day, the dogs know. They get super excited and throw themselves at the front door in eagerness, just to make sure I don't forget them. I often pack my car up the night before and my Toy Poodle will just hang around my hallway looking at me and then looking at the door, as if to say, 'Are we going yet?'

You and your dog can have real adventures together – meet new people, make new friends, get sporty (or not, if that's not your thing). I believe there is something for everyone, regardless of your personal (or your dog's) abilities. So if you don't like running but your dog does, canicross may not be for you – but what about flyball (more on these two below)? Whatever you're into, there is honestly a hobby out there that you can do with your dog, whether from your own home and garden or further afield. Read on for ideas; and to find a club or class for your chosen joyful activity, have a search online.

High-energy Sports

For the fitter dog who needs some extra spice in their life!

Agility training

One of the most popular sports for dogs is agility training, and the bonus is that there are many clubs offering this all over the country. It's high-energy – leaping over jumps, balancing on the seesaw and learning the tricky weave poles. And the great thing is it's a sport for dogs of all sizes. But it does require some running around on your part. It's really fun and the dogs who take part in the sport absolutely love it.

Agility training is fantastic for your relationship with your dog, and it really challenges them to use their minds (and their agility, obviously) to navigate the course. So it's a mental and physical workout. It's not suitable for young dogs who are still developing, though, due to all the jumping involved (see box on next page); nor is it good for older or disabled dogs.

Hoopers

Hoopers is a relatively new sport on the scene and, unlike agility, it's a sport for all dogs of all ages and all people of any fitness level – so even puppies, as well as older and disabled dogs (so long as they are reasonably fit and well) can take part, as the whole course is at ground level. It really makes the dog look to you for guidance, as it involves a lot of distance work, steering them around a course of tunnels and arches at speed. It's loads of fun, and without all the jumping around there is no repetitive damage to their joints.

A NOTE ON EXERCISING PUPPIES

When a puppy's bones are still growing and forming, you need to keep an eye on how much they jump and exercise, as this can cause bone and joint problems, particularly in larger breeds. Limit jumping on and off furniture and racing up and down stairs, for example, to protect them. A good rule of thumb for exercising pups is no more than five minutes for each month of their age, twice a day. So that's ten minutes for a two-month-old puppy and thirty minutes maximum for a six-month-old (and less for a large breed). Also, be mindful of how much running around they have been doing in your house and garden, too – this should all be taken into consideration.

Dogs are regarded as fully grown when they are one year old.

Flyball

Flyball is really gaining popularity and it's perfect for the speediest dogs. It's high-octane energy and, although it requires lots of training from you, you aren't required to run the course as you would with agility. The dogs are pumped to do it. They love it, running a straight race over hurdles to retrieve a tennis ball and bringing it back as fast as possible in a team relay race. Super fun to watch if you ever have the chance and a fabulous team activity.

IPO

IGP (Internationale Gebrauchshund Pruefung), previously known as IPO or Schutzhund, is one for the larger breeds (especially popular with the Dobermann and German Shepherd community). It uses tracking, obedience and protection training to test your dog's character and physical strength in a series of challenges. It's pretty competitive, so not one for the faint hearted.

As you know, my first dog was a Dobermann, and she came from a long line of IPO or Schutzhund champions, although I never looked into the sport myself.

Water sports

Do you have a water-loving hound? One that makes a beeline for any water whatsoever, be it a puddle or a lake? Well, dock diving (or jumping) is a sport in which dogs compete at jumping for distance or height from a dock into a body of water. It is incredible fun for that fearless leaper who throws themselves into the river in sheer joy. They look so hyped, living their best life.

Canicross

Like things more fast-paced? If your dog loves to run, or perhaps they are a breed designed to pull things (like a sled dog) or one with serious stamina (like a Dalmatian), canicross could be right up their street.

Canicross, which is really popular all over Europe, is a cross-country run where you wear a waist harness with your dog's lead attached, so that they are running out in front of you. You and your pooch are a team, and you guide them using verbal cues. So you need to train your dog to know their left from their right (this is a problem for me, as I still need to pretend to have a pen in my hand to know the difference). Plus, your dog has to be trained to run out in front of you (although running to the side is acceptable, too).

This is a sport suitable for fully grown dogs only, due to the duration of the runs and the impact on growing bones. You can also team dogs up, so, if you have two, you can train them to run with you together. Whether you have the racing bug or just want to do it for kicks, it looks like great fun. As for me – I avoided cross-country running at school like the plague and think I always will!

Bikejoring

If you enjoy picking up the pace on two wheels rather than two feet, check out Bikejoring. It's like canicross but on your bike. Its origins are in mushing but, in the absence of snow and a sled, you can use a bike and a harness instead. As with canicross, you need to train your dog with directional commands and safety around the bike before taking to the pedal. Typically, the word 'gee' is used for right and 'haw' for left (they are old terms used to steer horses). Plus, you also need to train your dog to start, slow down and stop.

It is a competitive sport, but if you love mountain biking and being out with your active and fit adult dog, it seems a great sport to get into. A variation is skijoring, where you are on skis and your dog pulls you along. Definitely one for me. If you are blessed to live in an area where snow is the norm and you love to cross-country ski, you'll love it, too. Imagine being towed around by your best pal – amazing!

Parkour

Ever heard of parkour, where gazelle-like humans effortlessly leap from wall to window to lamp post to railings in some real-life version of *Spider-Man*? Well, there's a dog version, too.

Dogs, being the agile ninjas they are, love the mental and physical challenge of an assault course (the exception being my mum's dog, who lazes around with the inclination to move of a sea slug). So if your dog has cat-like tendencies, check out parkour for dogs. You don't need any specialist equipment and it's an amazing workout for both body and brain.

Parkour is like high-intensity interval training using tree stumps, walls and beams and whatever else you see around you. Apparently, twenty minutes' worth of parkour work is equivalent to an hour's run. It encourages you to really look at your environment and utilise it to the full. An ordinary wall is suddenly a vehicle for gravity-defying parallel walking, while a tree stump becomes something to leap and balance on and a picnic bench is a hurdle to leap over.

OBEDIENCE WORK

If you are interested in more classical training, obedience work is very popular and pretty handy if your dog likes to take you for a walk rather than the other way around. You can work through classifications from puppy to bronze, silver then gold, and you can even get competitive.

Obedience work can be started as soon as your puppy can mix with other dogs and there are many clubs around, so your dog can meet some new pals and so can you. You start with basics like name recognition and recall and work through your badges: at bronze you work on your loose-lead walking, moving through gates in a steady manner and being controlled around other people and dogs. Then you move on to silver, where you need to continue working on everything you've previously done but to a more advanced level – like coming away from a distraction, road walking and entering and exiting a vehicle. For gold, you practise heel work off the lead, staying in one place and sending the dog to bed, to name a few. The training equips your dog for life with humans and exercises their mind at the same time. All training should be completely reward based and it helps you to form a great bond with your dog.

If you want to turn that obedience work up a notch and you love a kitchen disco, add some music to the training and try out heel work to music. It's mad, fun and hilarious to watch and seems to have a devoted following.

Ring craft

Have you got a pedigree dog who's a looker? If so, check out ring craft – show training for your handsome hound. There are many clubs where you can meet show folk, but it's also a great way of socialising your dog in a safe and controlled environment and also getting them used to being handled, which is so important.

I have attended ring-craft clubs for many many years, and, even if you don't fancy taking it to the next level and actually entering a dog show, it's great for your dog to mix with others of all ages, sizes and breeds. With dwind-ling numbers of pedigree dogs on the show circuit and terrible numbers of certain breeds now owned, especially in the UK, where some of our native breeds are on the crit-ical list as so few are being bred, it's great to get out there and support and show off your breed.

Non-sporting Activities

Hobbies and activities don't just have to be about sports clubs or getting competitive. There are so many things you can do with your dog within your four own walls or out on walks – so whether you have a rescue who is settling in and needs work around groups of dogs or you live in a remote area and don't have easy access to clubs and classes, there is still so much enrichment you can offer them.

Hydrotherapy

Hydrotherapy isn't only for rehabilitation, although, yes, it's a wonderful way to build strength post-surgery and help dogs with disabilities. It's also an amazing activity for improving physical stamina and building up strength and is fabulous for super-active and sporting dogs, too, enhancing condition and overall performance. But above all, it's a joyful way to exercise your pooch.

A hydrotherapy pool has currents in the water for the dog to swim with and against, providing resistance, so that just a few moments of swimming become a real workout. Using toys and encouragement, your dog will get much better at swimming, gain strength safely and have fun all at the same time. If you wish to try it out, if it's for medical reasons you will typically need veterinary consent and/or a referral.

Instagram

Have you ever thought about your pooch becoming an Instagram model? This is very twenty-first-century, and who would have thought it, but some people devote all their free time – even their careers – to focusing on their pup's fame, travelling with them, setting up photoshoots and being doggy influencers. It's not for every pup – only the most gregarious who love meeting new people and new four-legged friends. And, as we know, socials can take up a lot of your time. But it does mean you are going on new adventures with your bestie, visiting new places and having loads of fun along the way. So if you have a dog who loves the limelight, it could be a cool new hobby for the two of you to enjoy.

Trick training

This is a hoot – one that not only gets your dog's cogs whirring but is also fabulous to show other people. There are the usuals – paw or shake, then high five – but you can get pretty advanced with this stuff, too. Using your dog's treats as lures or training them to use a target stick, you can go crazy on the trick training.

Have you ever just got settled on the sofa and realised you don't have the remote control? Or you need to empty the washing machine, want a drink from the fridge or need to put something in the bin? I mean your dog isn't your personal assistant, but for fun you can teach them to do all these things. Crazy, right.

You can also train them to put themselves to bed, with a blanket, play dead, say their prayers, go fetch a specific object or do a commando roll. The list is endless, and they can build up a pretty large repertoire. I read about one dog who was able to distinguish between over 1,000 different objects (the Border Collie's guardian was a psychology professor who wanted to work out just how clever his canine was); pretty astounding, and it goes to show just how underworked our dogs' brains probably are.

'Hide and seek'

You can play games with your fuzz head, too. For this one, your dog needs to know a basic 'wait' cue.

With your dog lying in front of you, take three cups and hide a treat under one of them. Ask your dog to wait and then find it. Once the dog 'gets' it, you can start to mix the cups up like a magician and ask them to show you where the treat is. It gets them thinking, watching, waiting, sniffing; and you are interacting together in a different way from the higher-energy activities.

Does your dog have a favourite toy? You can use it to play a game of hide and seek in the house or garden. Start easy, asking them to sit and wait, then place the toy with them watching before asking them to find it. Then you can incrementally increase the difficulty level, so that it's further away and then out of sight, but continue to use the word 'find'. When they do find their toy, reward them with a game of tug.

Flirt poles

Flirt poles seem to be popular at the moment. They look like something I used to play with my cats as a kid – a pole with something exciting attached at the end of some string. They are good for physical and mental exercise and really get your dog working on their coordination and agility.

The flirt pole can also be used to train your dog (but don't tell them that – it should just be fun, as far as they are concerned, and exciting time spent with you), teaching them impulse control and helping them to tune out distractions and focus on you.

Toys and puzzles

I love an interactive toy and, if you do, too, there are lots of rope/tug toys, hide-and-seek toys, small toys you hide inside other toys and fuzzy lure toys on the market.

I am, or should I say my dogs are, the proud owners of an extensive array of puzzle toys (see p. 38). I bought my first about ten years ago when they were new on the market. I saw them at a dog exhibition and had high hopes for my dogs enjoying them. I wasn't disappointed.

Scatter feeding

Feeding your dog doesn't have to just be about putting some dry biscuit in a bowl. With scatter feeding (see p. 141), it can become an activity in itself. As well as keeping dogs busy, it promotes natural behaviours, encouraging them to use their noses and hunt for their food. You can hide the food in piles around your home or scatter it in your garden. I love using snuffle mats, lick mats, KONG toys (made from rubber and very durable, with a hole in the middle designed for stuffing with food) and treat toys, too.

It can really be beneficial for feeding to be something your dog has to think about. Just make sure they don't get frustrated and, as with anything like this, it's good to keep an eye on things – there's always the possibility that a dog will want to chew up and eat the whole lick mat!

Good old-fashioned walks

Going back to basics, if you don't choose to do any activities or hobbies with your dog, the minimum you should be doing for their mental health is enrichment on their walks. Their mental wellbeing is important, as we've seen, and dogs, like humans, can get bored.

Offer a variety of walking spots in different terrains – fields, woodlands, the beach and lakesides (see p. 123). Allow them to sniff and take their time, to just sit and be; let them feel comfortable leaving your side and exploring on their own, safely within range, but freely.

On walks, keep checking in with them, interacting, too. Take uphill walks together and enjoy a drink and a snack at a pub afterwards – the two of you.

All the activities we've looked at here will not only cement your bond with your dog but have a knock-on effect on your day-to-day life together. A more contented dog – a mentally

Mindful tip

When I'm out with my dogs and they are romping around, their joy increases tenfold if I join in with them, playing chase and running away, for example. Why not give this a try? Ignore whatever else is going on around you and just think about your dog – what are they feeling, hearing, seeing? – and feel a happy appreciation for the shared joy.

fulfilled and happy one – won't be expressing those barky attention-seeking behaviours at home or out and about. They will learn patience and obedience and, basically, how to put up with us (but in a fun and positive way).

I hope this has given you some ideas on how you might think beyond just another walk to the local park and back, to enhance your dog's life and, by extension, your relationship with them.

Holiday Time

You deserve a break – you really do. But what about Fido? You may prefer to take them everywhere with you or you may want a week just sunning yourself on a beach, away from everything.

Dog-free holidays

The thing I always think about is that if I am away having a jolly old time, I really want my dogs to have a jolly old time, too. Even if it does mean them staying in Blighty.

So if you have booked your holiday and it's not a dog-friendly one, what are the options for your pooch?

Kennels

I am not a fan of most kennels, and there are very few I would be comfortable leaving my dogs at. Having said that, my view is probably coloured by experiences with kennels many years ago; I know there are some very fancy hotel-like ones nowadays.

If you are lucky enough to live near (and be able to afford) a luxury kennel and your dog doesn't get distressed being away from you and other family members, then I recommend you do a drop-by and ask to look around.

I have seen some kennels advertised online that look spectacular, with heated rooms and televisions! Gone are the prison-cell blocks and two very short walks in a gravel compound; instead, there are grass paddocks and play time. And there are cameras, too, so you can check in on your friend morning, noon and night.

There is no kennel directory, so if you can't afford a luxury kennel and are unable to use any of the other services mentioned here, my advice is to do the legwork and look around some facilities to check they are clean and up to scratch.

Pet sitters

If your dog doesn't socialise well with other dogs and will get anxiety from being in a kennel environment, a pet sitter might be a good alternative.

Pet sitters will take your dog into their own home while

you are away. Go for a recommendation, if possible, and visit them. Try to get a handle on their routine and personality and ask if you can do a trial, too, to see how your dog fits in with their household. You also want them to ask *you* lots of questions – about things like your dog's likes and dislikes, what and when you feed them, their usual routine, whether they socialise well with other dogs and where they like to sleep at night.

The advantage of this arrangement is that your dog has all the home comforts, makes new friends and has the company of humans. They should get good walks every day, too, and lots of interaction.

There are also approved pet sitters who will move into your home (see Resources, p. 248), so the dog is surrounded by their own home comforts, familiar smells and sights, just with a new buddy to take care of their needs. There are a few companies who will find you a pet sitter (see Resources, p. 248) but, again, I love a recommendation from someone I know who has used a similar service. I once used an in-house sitter and came back to a filthy home, which didn't please me at all. I'm sure this was just a one-off bad experience, but it does reinforce the fact that a recommendation is advisable.

Family and friends

Then there is the long-suffering family and friends list – the one that I love to exhaust! But having so many dogs does mean it's a big ask for someone to look after them for a week or two. Luckily for me, I have the best mama in the world, who will always take them in, or watch them if I'm out for too long.

You could also strike a deal with a friend who has a dog and agree that when they go away you will care for their dog and, in return, they will mind yours – a doggy swap that's mutually beneficial, and you know your dog will be well cared for and loved like one of their own.

And dog comes, too

What about travelling *with* your dog? Even on day trips your dog needs to be a safe and happy traveller.

Travelling by car
It's the law in the UK that your dog must not be loose in a vehicle. They must be either tethered in the back with a harness and seatbelt attachment or safely in the boot of the vehicle. Gone are the days of dogs catching flies as they hang out of the window, enjoying the wind in their chops! (Back in the day, I would have my two Dobermanns on the back seat of my vehicle: one out of each window – a pretty awesome sight to behold.)

My dogs all travel in the boot except for my little Toy, who likes to be in the centre of the vehicle, as she gets a little travel sick and that's where there is the least rocking and swaying movement.

Small dogs generally feel better if they can look out of the window. You can get cute booster seats for dogs online or in pet stores, which you can safely secure them into as well. Now, on our trips out or on holiday, we have a poodle in a booster seat sandwiched between two small children, with

> **TRAVEL TIP**
>
> If your dog suffers from severe travel sickness, don't feed them too close to travelling time. Instead, get up early and feed them two to three hours before you set off, or wait until you have arrived. You can also speak to your vet about travel-sickness tablets.

three little faces peeping out of the windows. Hilarious!

In the car I always make sure I have plenty of fresh water, a water bowl and my biodegradable poop bags. I also have spare leads, just in case one of us forgets to pack them, plenty of towels, the dogs' collars with my details on their tags and a first-aid kit containing the following:

- Tweezers
- Tick-removal tool
- Different-sized bandages
- Self-adhesive bandage or Vetrap
- Sting relief
- Cleaning fluid/ antiseptic wash
- Safety pins

- Blunt-ended scissors
- Cotton wool
- Surgical tape
- Thick towel or large blanket (suitable to be used as a stretcher)
- Elizabethan collar
- Foil blanket

My dogs are seasoned travellers, as I drive them around so much for work and for dog shows, so they are all pretty calm in the car. If your dog isn't used to it, however – especially long journeys to go on holiday – you don't want what should be a lovely time away to be spoiled by stress and anxiety, panting, dribbling and dread. So try desensitising your pooch to the car: take them on small journeys to start with, creating plenty of positive associations (like going to preferred local walking haunts) and build up from there.

You can also ask your vet for some calming medication if their anxiety is severe, or look at natural alternatives like valerian compound, which can be purchased from any dog herbalist.

Caravanning

Ever thought about taking your dog camping or caravanning? Well, you wouldn't be the only one. Camp sites are really dog-friendly places and lots of families take their dogs with them.

I have a tent that is plenty big enough for my children, my dogs and all our clobber. I make sure I have extra bedding for the dogs, lots of towels, tie-out stakes that corkscrew into the ground and a bedding area (both inside the caravan and under the awning, so that when they are outside they can be away from the main footpaths where fellow campers continually pass by), providing safe spaces for them to hang out in. I also have a sort of pop-up seaside umbrella that's made of reflective material, which offers them protection from sun, rain and wind – so whatever the weather, there is dry shelter for them. (But more likely than not, you, like many a camper, will end up going home with a wet dog and a damp tent.)

A wonderful plus to having a dog with you when you go away is you get to chat to so many lovely dog folk, but do bear in mind that not everyone loves dogs, and a lot of people may not be as overcome with happiness as you are at your dog leaping around barking and catching bubbles with your children at 8am on a Sunday. So be respectful towards others and keep your pal under control. No one appreciates a morning wake-up from a yapping Jack Russell or a rampaging damp Labrador pouncing on their tent or pinching their picnic.

Here are my tips for camping, caravanning and motor-homing with your dog:

🐾 Ensure they are suitably restrained in the car or motorhome.

🐾 Ensure the information on their microchip is up to date.

- Stock up on their food and treats.

- Plan your trip, schedule rest breaks and look for dog-friendly places to eat, have a drink and walk.

- Don't leave your pet unattended.

- Pack your dog's first-aid kit (see p. 213 for what this should include).

- Don't forget their lead and collar/harness, their bowls, toys and lots of poo bags (for the dog who likes to pee or 'mark' everything, a short lead is a must).

- Respect the rules of the site – usually dogs are always on a lead.

- Take some towels for muddy paws and soggy days.

- Ensure they have shade when outside (a canopy or sunshade).

- Check their flea and tick treatments are up to date.

- A waterproof bed is a great investment, as you can wipe the dirt off.

- Take blankets for colder nights.

- Remember a tie-out hook.

Holidays abroad with your dog

The passport situation for dogs differs from country to country. In the UK, the laws have changed since we left the European Union and it's now more expensive to get your

TOP TIPS FOR HOLIDAYING WITH YOUR DOG IN YOUR OWN COUNTRY

The key here is planning. Consider the following:

- Is the local pub/café where you are planning to hang out dog friendly?

- What are the local walks like and are they dog friendly? I went somewhere recently where you weren't allowed to take dogs on a lot of the walks, as it was ground-bird nesting season and the area was protected. This can also apply to a lot of beaches.

- Make sure your dog is healthy and fit to travel.

- Check that the information on your dog's tag is up to date and their microchip is working.

- Stock up on all your dog's food and treats.

dog passport sorted. There's lots of useful information about this online (see Resources, p. 248) and about travelling abroad with your dog in general. Just be sure to read the rules properly.

I have taken my dogs to France multiple times, and it was much easier than I thought it would be. I also found that restaurants, cafés and bars on the Continent were much more dog friendly than here in England, which is strange, given that the UK is a dog-loving nation. We had no issues finding dog-friendly hotels and were surprised at how easy the Eurotunnel crossing was with dogs – there is even an exercise area for them to stretch their legs in and toilet before embarking.

Make sure you are aware of any potential health risks for your dog before you travel to another country. For example, the ticks can be bad in the south of France, so we kitted our dogs out with tick collars as an extra precaution. The vets in France seemed clued up on the requirements to re-enter the UK for our dogs and it was all pretty streamlined. They knew what needed to be done with my dogs' paperwork and worming/ tick treatment for our return to the UK and were so accommodating. Plus, I was ready with my French–English dictionary in hand, but it was fine – their English was embarrassingly brilliant!

Different countries pose different health risks, so the best idea is to speak to your own vet or a local vet in the place you are travelling to for advice.

Whichever route you choose, the important thing when you're planning a trip is that your dog is safe and has an amazing time with lots of new adventures – whether they are travelling with you or having their own holiday without you.

TIP

We have found a cool coat – a faux chamois cloth made into a dog coat – to be a brilliant investment. You put it in cold water (or you can even freeze it) and it stays cool and wet for a long time, reducing your dog's body temperature. Short-nosed, heavy-coated and elderly dogs in particular can easily overheat, so this is a great idea for them.

12

BONDING

I've talked a lot about your relationship with your dog and the bond you should share but, in this chapter, we will look at specific bonding activities and practices, and why building that relationship of trust and connection is so important for a happy dog and a happy you.

Dogs have been proven to be good for our health, and scientists increasingly recognise how much they have to offer us, giving us purpose, unconditional love and emotional support. Playing with your dog can elevate levels in the body of serotonin and dopamine, which serve to relax you, while spending time with them activates the same neural pathways in the brain that are stimulated in a parent by a baby. They raise our levels of oxytocin (also known as the love hormone), helping to alleviate stress. They also calm us down and help with depression and anxiety, not to mention loneliness. And that's before we even get to the physical benefits associated with walking and exercising them.

During the pandemic there was a huge rise in dog guardianship. Dogs really were the unsung heroes during those difficult times, getting us out of the house, offering company and a snuggly body to lift our moods after our daily dose of depressing news.

More people than ever are now proud guardians of a dog and I think most will never look back. The joy our dogs bring to our lives is second to none and they deserve to be treated like the kings and queens they are. They don't interfere with our choice of partners or housemates, they don't judge us, so long as we are always kind and understanding towards them, and they don't discriminate if we are disabled. And they are always delighted to make tasks that are tricky for someone easier when they can, as we see with disability therapy dogs and guide dogs. They are endlessly giving, selfless creatures. It's love, pure and simple.

A NEW LEASE OF LIFE

I recently read a news article about a high-flying businessman who pushed life to the limit, worked tirelessly and rarely had time for himself or his loved ones. One day, he woke up, started crying and couldn't stop. He lost the ability to string a sentence together, couldn't contemplate work or even get out of bed. He credits his recovery (aside from any professional help and a change of job) to the little rescue dog he got. She gave him a reason to get out of bed, get out into the fresh air and go walking every day, putting one foot in front of the other. Over time, he started to appreciate his walks, as they lifted his spirits. The small dog who, it turns out, rescued *him*, had a wonderful effect on his mental health and so the recovery began.

Dogs can offer a lifeline to anyone who is isolated, getting them out and about, mixing in society and meeting new people, or just simply offering them a change from their norm.

Working on Your Special Bond

Forming a connection is not instantaneous. The love and devotion are there from the moment you first give them a hug and a sniff (that's if you are like me and also love sniffing puppies). But that human-to-dog connection takes time, work and patience – on both parts. *You* need to be patient when they dig a hole in your rug and piddle on your floor for the fiftieth time; and *they* need to be patient trying to understand the busy and complex world they find themselves in.

A connection with your dog is more than just peering into their eyes and speaking to their soul. It's about understanding each other, each of you knowing how the other will react, how to read situations and be kind and tolerant always. Here are some ways to help you achieve that unbreakable bond.

- **Spend quality time together** – going on new adventures, walking your favourite walks, watching your top TV shows in each other's company, laughing (well, you will be laughing; your dog may just look at you or lick you if they agree).

- **Put thought into their food** – don't just throw dry, low-quality kibble into their bowl. Think about the nutrition they are getting. As previously mentioned, you are what you eat, and that applies to your dog, too, so feed them with love, with variety and excitement – like an Italian grandmother.

- **Think about their likes and dislikes** – if you know they hate going out for walks in the rain, don't force it just to tick a box. Two of my dogs hate the rain, so on wet days, we play games, have fun indoors, cuddle and wait for a break in the clouds, alongside working on desensitising them to rain. I see so many miserable-looking dogs soaked to the bone out on their road plods because they need a walk. And I get it if you have to work and need to get them out first, but at least put a raincoat on the rain haters. Conversely, if their favourite thing in the whole world is running on a beach and throwing seaweed into the air, try to set some weekends aside for beach days. They will think they have gone to heaven.

- 🐾 **Be a calm leader, not a dictator** – be the guiding hand that makes them feel secure and the safe arms they can come to when they are unsure. Don't smother them either; they are dogs, after all, and, even though they might sometimes need some reassurance, they shouldn't be mollycoddled. Read the situation and learn to read your dog, too. I often see guardians displaying over-the-top dog parenting, worrying and smothering, but it's all about energy and confidence and knowing where to draw the line.

- 🐾 **Set aside time for quiet cuddles** or their preferred form of affection – do they love their belly scratched or their ears diddled? Animals bond over that close relationship – licking, picking, tending to each other's coats, playing and snuggling up together. So an easy way to bond with your dog is to 'just be' with them (hard work, isn't it?).

- 🐾 **Think about their needs** (as opposed to your own) – for example, we all need some time and space occasionally, don't we? Perhaps you have a hectic household like mine, with lots going on at any given time . . . It's an assault on the senses, and some dogs just want quiet time.

🐾 **Remember their sleep requirements** – dogs sleep a lot (a fulfilled dog should sleep about thirteen out of every twenty-four hours), so allow them to do that – encourage it, even. If you can, set aside a quiet den space they can take themselves off to, away from the clatter of pans and flying crayons.

🐾 **Remind your children to be considerate** – make sure they aren't harassing the dog when they are quietly relaxing; or any time, really, but especially when they are in their quiet spot. Teaching all your family to respect the dog's space is vital to earning their trust in all of you.

🐾 **Learn to recognise and interpret their vocalisations** – because you wouldn't necessarily think it, but dogs often develop their own way of trying to talk to us. Chirrups, whines, yips and barks are your dog's way of talking, and understanding the slight variations can help you to identify whether they are instigating play, showing frustration, offering/needing comfort. When one of my dogs curls up with me, they mumble away with contentment. And my old Dobermann used to moan like an old fishwife when our dinner was served and I asked her to sit in her bed.

Your bond with your dog will come on in leaps and bounds if you are conscious of all the above and mindful of their needs, letting them know just how important they are to you.

BONDING THROUGH GROOMING

Like petting your dog, grooming is a way of cementing your bond with them. Taking time to brush them and comb their locks is very much an act of love. Have you seen how wolves groom each other to strengthen their family bond? They will lick and nibble at each other's coats to remove debris and to clean them, but it is also a way of showing love. Wolves also greet each other by wet nosing and licking each other's faces, much like our domesticated dogs. For them, it's instinctual, but this touch, whether as a form of greeting or grooming, also provides security, comfort and love.

Getting Close to Your Dog

Being close to your dog reduces levels of cortisol, the hormone responsible for stress and anxiety – something we are all aware of nowadays. But it's mutually beneficial, too – because they feel the same effects as we do.

Cuddles

A cuddle has to be on the dog's terms. Mine rarely miss an opportunity for a hug, unless they are waiting to play or eat their dinner. But a rescue dog, for example, may well be stressed out by being cuddled before they have cemented their bond with you and feel a good level of trust. So don't push yourself on a dog – let them come to you for cuddle time.

Cuddles have wonderful benefits for your dogs, reducing

cortisol levels and making them feel good. When a dog accepts a cuddle, it means they trust you and consider you to be part of their close-knit group.

If your dog doesn't like cuddles, it can be because you are limiting their ability to run away (when dogs are scared, they like to feel that they can run away – it's instinctive). Some rescue and rehomed dogs also may have never learned to cuddle or could have been mishandled in the past. Or they may be in pain, which will make them wary of touch. If this is the case, you need to visit a vet and have that pain investigated and managed with medication.

Uncuddly dogs *can* become cuddly, but you need to work on their trust and their bond with you. This takes time and patience and should always be on their terms, so that they feel in control. To start with, reduce your physical contact with the dog for two or three days and simply read their body language – see if they start to request contact from you by coming up to you and placing their head on you, for example, or leaning on you. Use lots of play, praise and training and, when they do seem to want attention, don't envelop them with your arms – start by slowly stroking them, tickling them, gradually building up that trust.

Eye contact

Eye contact with dogs is a hotly debated topic. Is it a bonding exercise or not? Well, it depends on who's giving the direct eye contact to your dog. If it's another dog or a stranger, it can be unnerving. (Their ancestor, the wolf, would consider direct eye contact a threat and some dogs still have this opinion.) But dogs are pros at adapting and have learned over generations of breeding for pets that eye contact isn't always threatening and can sometimes be quite the opposite. The right eye contact from the right person at the right time can trigger a release of oxytocin (that love hormone), helping with communication and building a bond. (A study in Japan in 2015 showed that following direct eye contact between dogs and their guardians, there was a 130 per cent rise in oxytocin in the dogs and a huge 300 per cent in their guardians.[3]) I remember my mum telling me how her dog stares at her and it feels like she's touching her soul.

But aside from the physiological effects of eye contact, it's also a form of communication. My mum's dog, for example, will stare at her when she wants something, and the moment my mum locks eyes with her she will, say, look in the direction of her dinner bowl and then back at my mum and back and forth, letting her know, in the clearest way possible, that she wants some dinner. She also does this when she wants to go outside, as do my own dogs, who will loiter by the door, taking it in turns to stare me down and then pivoting to stare at the door. They are saying, 'Come on, let us out,' but, if I'm busy rushing around, it's easy to miss this, so I'm training them to use door bells (those sleigh bells on a long line) that they knock to make a sound.

Take some time out to lie on the floor with your dog and enjoy a minute of eye contact and see how it makes you feel.

A bonding massage

One activity that costs absolutely nothing but your time is dog massage. This is wonderful for increasing their circulation, and the oxygenated blood travelling around their body has rejuvenating properties. You can also carry out a thorough health test as you massage, feeling for any anomalies; plus, it releases endorphins, helping to calm you both down and lowering blood pressure. But perhaps best of

---

3   https://www.science.org/doi/full/10.1126/science.1261022

all, a massage works wonders for strengthening that bond between the two of you.

So even for those of you who don't see yourselves rolling out the blanket and playing whale sounds, the physical contact with your dog will help to relax you both, as well as being a beautiful bonding exercise and one built on trust. For full instructions on how to do a dog massage, see pp. 155–158.

Games

Your dog can't join you in a family game of Monopoly or share your children's skipping rope, but dogs do love games. You can even get the whole family involved in spending quality time with Fido. As well as offering enrichment to the dog, this also teaches children about the responsibility of caring for an animal and how meeting their needs goes beyond food and shelter. Here are some ideas:

- **Fetch** Probably the most common game played with dogs, and mine love it, but I do have to keep it to a minimum as one of my dogs is ball obsessed.

- **Hide and seek** An oldie but goodie, and one we play in our house seemingly daily, as my kids love it; and dogs can, too. I use their favourite toy and make the game increasingly difficult once they have grasped the idea (see p. 206). We also play hide and seek with the dogs themselves in our house and garden; the dogs learn to tune in to their senses of smell and hearing to hunt us down. It's hilarious to do, as long as they feel secure and understand it's a game. You don't want to induce any panic.

- 🐾 **Flirt poles** I mentioned these earlier (see p. 207); just a few minutes of playing with one of these offers the same mental stimulation as a walk.

- 🐾 **Tug of war** This is another classic. My dogs love a game of tug of war and their tug toys are probably their most favoured. It's great physical exercise for them and they play tug with each other, too.

- 🐾 **Agility course** Another fun activity that all the family can get involved in is making your own agility course in your garden, using hula hoops, cones, planks of wood and blankets, for example.

Play – using any of the above suggestions or others – is a gorgeous way of cementing your bond with your dog. It really makes them happy and fulfilled, as long as they don't get overaroused or frustrated with the game (keep an eye out for this via signs in their body language – they will be unable to settle or calm themselves down, they may grab at things, be super mouthy, tremble, pant, lick, zoom around or bark incessantly). Also, remember to let the dog win! If you win it only makes the dog frustrated (and if anyone has ever told you that you must win as a show of your dominance, that's another one of those myths). Their reward for playing and interacting is to win the toy and to play with you.

The possibilities are endless and the fun limitless. And when are you happiest? When those around you are at their happiest, right?

What We Can Learn From Our Dogs

Dogs can teach us a lot about how we can improve our lives in this crazy, fast-paced world we live in. And we can help them – and all those around us – by becoming the zen guardians of dogs, through our positive energy and mindful outlook.

Empathy and Forgiveness

These are an important part of leading a fulfilling life. We are all taught to practise forgiveness, but how many of us do?

Dogs don't hold on to sadness, anger, bitterness and neither should we. But they are feeders on our energy and emotions, emulating the energy we give off and mirroring our behaviour, so we need to be mindful of this, taking steps to be calm, so that this is the vibe our dogs sense and mirror. This can improve your dog's wellbeing and state of mind, and yours as well.

Dogs don't care about how you look or what you wear.

All they care about is you and your happiness. Be proud, accept you for you, be real and love who you are – not an enhanced version of yourself.

Tell people you love them and that you appreciate them, in the same way your dog tells you every time they look at you. Being intimate and loving is something a dog always demonstrates, be that dog to human or dog to dog. That connection is so beautiful, releasing endorphins and good energy, and it makes us realise what truly is important.

Positive attitude

Attitude is everything. And dogs, for the most part, have tremendous attitudes.

A good attitude can take you places. It can turn a bad situation into a learning experience and will even alter your mood. Try greeting everyone with joy, for example, and see how that sunshine reflects right back at you. Be doglike in your enthusiasm for the world. Be curious, interested and enthusiastic, without preconceived ideas, like a dog tearing on to a new beach. It's amazing how differently a scenario can play out when we turn our attitude on its head and are simply more dog.

There are so many ways in which you can bond with a new dog and cement your bond with an existing dog. Remember, bonding is mutually beneficial and just great for the soul – communication and understanding between the two of you will be clearer and allow your dog to feel comfortable and safe in your presence. You can't wish for much more than that.

HYGGE

Hygge is a Danish word for cosiness, being snuggly and comfortable, appreciating the simple things in life and cherishing moments of peace, whether with friends or at home. Hygge is widely regarded as being beneficial for us, promoting relaxation, making our minds and bodies feel good and giving us that feeling of safety within our environments.

Dogs are the perfect hygge partners – in the UK, we have pretty long, cold winters and dogs are the epitome of snuggliness, cosiness and comfort. So whether you want to curl up together beside a fire enjoying a cosy night in, pop on your snuggliest jumper and head out on a winter walk or cook something warm and hearty that you can both enjoy, make sure you take time to cosy up, switch off and relax in each other's embrace.

Here are some tips for living a cosy hygge lifestyle with our dogs:

- 🐾 **Spend quality time with family and friends** (both four- and two-legged), whether you're popping in for a coffee, indulging in a box-set binge or having a cosy candlelit dinner party.

- 🐾 **Eat well.** On a cold day, eat something that warms the soul (your dog's, too). Hygge is sometimes described as 'healthy hedonism', so to me that would mean a slug of wine and a delicious cheese board.

- 🐾 **Wear comfortable clothing.** That doesn't mean you turn into a complete slob, but wear things that are warm, cosy and relaxing, ditching the tight waistbands or formal shirts. And the dog equivalent would be removing their collar after a walk – they must be pretty annoying, after all, jangling around their necks, tag clinking away all the time.

- 🐾 **Get on your bike!** The Danes love to cycle but if the prospect doesn't fill you with joy (as is the case for me in my hilly, busy town), try some other form of exercise, taking your dog out with you (see Chapter 11 for inspiration) and breathing in that fresh air.

- 🐾 **Avoid multitasking.** You may be a whizz when it comes to multitasking, but if you are watching a film or spending time with loved ones and you keep checking your emails or your phone, that's not good hygge practice. Concentrate on your leisure time in leisure time, not what's happening tomorrow or at work next week. Be present, like a dog.

- 🐾 **Address your work/life balance.** Leave work at an appropriate time and don't bring it home with you. I'm a fine one to talk, as you'll often find me, laptop in hand at ten in the evening – and it really irritates my husband, too. We all know this isn't healthy practice, so close the laptop, leave work at work and plan some down time instead – time with friends or snuggling into your dog on the sofa, under a throw, drinking hot chocolate.

🐾 **Eradicate stress.** Stress is no one's friend – it keeps us awake at night and even shortens our life-spans. Try to remove anything from your situation that makes you feel stressed. You don't want to feel annoyed, sad or overwhelmed when you are practising hygge (or ever). Putting these emotions to bed, even temporarily, will really help you to relax and unwind.

If our dogs could run our lives, I'm pretty sure they would be all about hygge!

13

OLD AGE

It creeps up on us all, and, having been a pet parent to many an older dog, I know how tough it can be seeing your dog decline as old age sets in.

Older age for a dog starts at around seven years, but it really is breed dependent. For a Great Dane, for example, life expectancy is much shorter than it is for a Yorkshire Terrier. I have known giant breeds to pass away at nine years, just through old age, and I used to groom a twenty-one-year-old Border Terrier – he was white all over through age, like a little wise old man. The oldest dog known to exist was an Australian Cattle Dog called Bluey, who lived until he was nearly thirty and worked for twenty years of his life on a ranch. What a dog!

Spotting the Signs

What signs do you need to look out for to tell you that your dog is entering their senior years? Well, they may start with some lumps and bumps over their body, or you may notice their coat isn't growing as fast as it used to, and it can also appear dull and may be greying around their muzzle. They can lose weight and start to change body shape, their feet may show signs of arthritis (see below), their spines can sink more due to spondylosis and their walk may not be as bouncy as before.

There will be behavioural changes, too. They may not be able to keep up on their walks and, if they overdo it, they will be slow and stiff the next day. They can also seem more lethargic and reluctant to participate in the play and fun they used to love so much. My older dogs have good days and slower days.

Here are some of the main issues that can arise:

- **Arthritis** This can be seen as joint stiffness, especially in the colder months. Your dog may be reluctant to go for walks and take time to get out of bed. It can be managed with supplements and visits to the vet for check-ups and medication, but taking them on shorter and more frequent walks is a good idea, and not pushing them to overexercise.

- **Overweight** Being porky and overweight puts additional pressure on your dog's joints and strain on their bodies, so keeping an optimum weight is important. If you are struggling with your dog's weight, speak to your vet – a lot have weight-loss clubs for dogs and can offer you advice on feeding, but unless it's a medical problem it is likely down to a lack of movement and overfeeding. So don't be taken in by those eyes – reducing those treats and big dinners really is the kindest thing you can do for them.

- **Stinky breath** This is not pleasant! If you get up close and personal with your pooch and there is a pong, it's a sign that all is not well with their gnashers. Small breeds in particular suffer with their teeth. Gum disease and tartar build up in your dog's mouth and, left untreated, it can be serious, as the infection can easily travel into their bones and, eventually, cause organ damage. Make sure you take a trip to the vet and have them assess your dog's teeth if there are any signs of decay or bad odour; they can advise you as to the best course of action.

- **Nail health** As dogs age, their gait (that's how they walk) may change and they will be running around less, so not wearing their nails down. It's important, therefore, to keep a check on them and make sure they are not too long, as this can further inhibit their movement. But what is too long? Well, if they are in the standing position and their nails are touching the floor, they are too long. Visit your groomer regularly to have them trimmed.

- **Doggy dementia** Yes, it's really a thing. My Dobermann suffered with dementia. As she got older, she would become confused and then have moments of clarity; she started to toilet in the house, and this would upset her greatly; she also started barking a lot (a strange bark – one that I hadn't heard from her before) and pacing around the house in circles. It was sad to see, but it's apparently quite common. I remember my nana's Norfolk Terrier would stare at the wall when she was old and suffering from Alzheimer's. If you notice any of these or other out-of-the-ordinary behaviours, speak to your vet for advice on managing dementia in dogs.

- **Deteriorating eyesight** There are many causes of sight loss in older dogs, including macular degeneration and glaucoma or cataracts. Signs to watch out for include clouding of the eye and struggling to see, particularly at night. Often, sight loss is gradual and you may not notice it until you take your dog to a new environment or decide to rearrange your furniture. If you have any concerns, your vet can inspect your dog's eyes for any problems. Managing sight loss isn't too hard, as long as you put the time in, and dogs can live a normal and full life with impaired vision or even complete sight loss. As their night vision deteriorates in their latter years, I leave a small light on for my dogs, and I always keep their food and water bowls in the same position.

🐾 **Hearing loss** This is another issue for the older dog. We always joke that my older Poodle has selective hearing (a bit like my grandad used to): she doesn't hear me coming into a room, but always hears her dinner bowl being put out! I started to notice her hearing was genuinely declining slightly when I would get up in the morning, clatter downstairs with the children in tow (ours isn't a quiet household) and all the dogs would be at the door excitedly greeting us except for old Lily Legs, who would still be fast asleep in her bed and would jump when I touched her, bless her. Perhaps she just sleeps much more deeply now she is older. But also, her recall was always on point, whereas now, on walks, she either can't hear me or just chooses to ignore me. Oh well, I suppose that's old-dog privileges – and she's never up to no good, just sniffing some really good sniffs.

🐾 **Lumps and bumps** Older dogs do get lumpy, and they can develop warts, too. If you spot a lump, go to your vet, as they can take a sample from it to make sure it is nothing sinister. Warts are caused by a virus and are contagious to other dogs (and they can spread on your dog's body, too). Older dogs are more prone to warts and they can even grow in their mouths and on their eyelids, causing them great discomfort. Apple cider vinegar can be used as a remedy to treat warts. Firstly, ensure that you use the raw, unfiltered kind. This can be applied directly to the wart/s on a cotton pad (don't use it near their eyes, though – warts on the eyes may need to be removed by a vet). Alternatively, you can add the vinegar to their food (1 teaspoon for dogs up to 7kg, 2 teaspoons for dogs weighing 8–16kg, 1 tablespoon for 17–38kg dogs). And while we're on the subject of apple cider vinegar, as it's natural and anti-microbial, it also has many other uses – for cleaning a dog's ears, helping with allergies, recovery from UTIs and improving gut health. As you would when trying anything new with your dog, internally or externally, monitor for any adverse reactions.

As your dog gets older, you may find yourself at the vet more frequently. It's just part and parcel of the ageing process and, as their guardian, you have a duty to look after them in their best years and in their twilight years. Do right by them and show your love by maintaining their health as best you can. Dogs have an uncanny ability to hide pain; it's a primeval behaviour inherited from their ancestors – not showing weakness, as this could make them easy targets for predators. So if you think something isn't right but your dog seems fine in themselves, don't take their word for it – they are masters of disguise.

Aside from seeking professional help, there are things you can do at home, too, to help an ageing pooch. I give mine glucosamine supplements to help with their joints, omega-3 oil, which is an anti-inflammatory, and a Keeper's Mix. The latter contains kelp, celery seeds and nettle, among other things, and helps with their skin, coat and overall health – you may need to wait a few months to notice the impact on your dog, but I highly recommend supporting them physically with the use of these supplements, especially glucosamine.

I don't put my dogs on to a senior diet but feed them in the same way I fed them as adults, with a raw and natural, balanced diet. I ensure they are getting all the nutrients they need and that the food I am giving them is of top quality. As I've said before, you are what you eat, and an older dog needs top-quality nutrition to keep everything functioning as it should.

THERAPIES

If you want to go the extra mile, there are lots of therapies you can try on your pooch:

- 🐾 **Hydrotherapy** I love hydrotherapy, and it's an especially popular choice for managing arthritis. The buoyancy from the water supports the dog, while they can build up muscle strength to support their joints and improve cardiac fitness.

- 🐾 **Acupuncture** A well-known Chinese therapy, dating back thousands of years, this is used to manage chronic pain in dogs. During an acupuncture session, tiny needles are inserted into certain sites on the dog's body to relieve specific symptoms, such as chronic pain, and to balance the flow of energy. To find a local specialist you can search canine acupuncture online or see Resources, p. 248.

Chiropractic This can be used for any mechanical problems with the dog's bones. I used a chiropractor for one of my oldies and noticed a significant improvement in her movement afterwards. They usually focus on the spine and work from there to improve mechanical function. To find your nearest qualified animal chiropractor, you can search online or see Resources, p. 248.

Physiotherapy Like hydrotherapy, this works to strengthen and build up your dog's range of movement and muscles. A physiotherapist will use exercises, manual manipulation and massage to improve function. Look for practitioners who are registered veterinary physiotherapists with the International Association for Animal Therapists (IAAT – see Resources, p. 248).

Other therapies Reiki and magnetic therapy can help to alleviate joint pain in oldies and to encourage faster recovery following surgery. Reiki uses energy transfer to heal (see p. 153), while magnetic therapy uses the power of the magnetic force.

Home Adjustments

In and around your home, there are adjustments you can make to help your ageing dog:

🐾 **The car** If you have a big dog that would previously bound in and out of your boot, and they are too heavy for you to lift on your own, invest in a ramp to help you both. This can be stowed away in your boot and it makes getting in and out of the vehicle less daunting for your dog.

🐾 **Sofas and beds** If your dogs are sofa surfers, a well-positioned pouffe can act as a step on to furniture. For their beds, though, I can't recommend a raised bed highly enough. Because these are higher off the ground, they make it easier for the dog to get in and out of bed. Plus, because they are raised, it means they are not sleeping on a cold, hard floor during the colder months, while in the warmer months the hammock style supports their joints and air can circulate around them more easily, keeping them cooler.

🐾 **Floors** If you have hard floors, you may notice your dog begins to slip around more on them and struggles with their footing. Some even develop a fear of walking on slippery surfaces, so consider placing runners and rugs down for them.

🐾 **Stairs** If your dog loves to follow you around your home, it's a good idea to limit opportunities for them to use the stairs by installing a gate, because the movement of coming down them can be difficult for older dogs.

- 🐾 **Going for walks** If you have a pack of dogs who love to go out together and you don't want your oldie to miss out, train them to use a doggy stroller or a pull-along cart – that way, you can still enjoy days out together without worrying that it's too far for them to walk. (The cart also doubles up as a child transportation system and everyone will want to jump in and dump their bits and bobs in, too!)

- 🐾 **Meals** As I mentioned earlier, always keep their food and water in the same place but change up their dishes for raised feeders. These are not only much better for barrel-chested dogs as they reduce the risk of bloat, but they also encourage a much more comfortable eating position for oldies.

- 🐾 **Comfort** If your dog is suffering from dementia-induced anxiety, a wrap vest is great. It's like a swaddle for dogs, providing constant gentle pressure, and it can reduce anxiety in some dogs – a bit like a reassuring cuddle.

- 🐾 **Night time** Eyesight deteriorates in old age, so pop a night light or a lamp on for them to make them feel more comfortable and better able to navigate the home.

- 🐾 **Toileting** Accidents can happen with older dogs, so get some puppy pee pads in and lay one by the door if your dog has started to urinate in the house. It will save your rugs, and you can get more environmentally friendly versions now that you can wash out and reuse.

When Is It Time to Say Goodbye?

Ultimately, there is no right time for us; it's going to be painful whenever it comes. But we have to put the dog first and deal with our own emotions afterwards. Dogs give us the blessing of their best years, with devoted love and loyalty, and now it's our time to make sure we look after them, so they have a peaceful and pain-free passing. This is the kindest thing we can do for our dogs.

With an older dog we need to take the time to watch and read their body language, look for subtle changes and keep them as happy and comfortable as they can be. But how do we know when it's time to say goodbye? I'm sure you, like me, would love for them to just pass away in their sleep, blissfully unaware and at peace. But the reality is that this rarely happens and we have to intervene before their well-being is compromised by poor health.

Old and poorly dogs can yo-yo from one day to the next, so that you make a decision that it's time to let them go, and then, as if by magic, they are tottering around again, enjoying breakfast and taking a turn in the garden. With my Dobermann, I booked in and cancelled appointments at the vet to have her put to sleep twice – she would be grand one day and then poorly the next.

So it's a fine line between the right time and leaving it that bit too long, but it's all about quality of life. Yes, your dog could go on for another year with that super-strong heart, but are they happy and pain free? When I was toying with what to do with Angel, I was told by a fantastic vet to look for a quality-of-life scale online (see Resources, p. 248). This gives scores for mobility, appetite, hydration, attitude, elimination (toileting) and favourite things, and you rate your dog every couple of days, using the scale provided, until it indicates that intervention is needed. You then have an overview of your dog's quality of life, letting you know whether they are ok for the time being, if intervention is required or humane euthanasia should be considered.

It really is such an emotive subject because it's you who has to make the decision, and it's always heartbreaking at the end. But you don't want to get to a point where your dog is really suffering. They can't understand why they feel the way they do, so you have to put your feelings aside and do what's right for them.

End of an Era

We need to deal with death in a conscious way – conscious of our dog's feelings and putting them first. We don't know exactly how they feel, other than by watching their body language, and even they themselves won't understand why they feel so poorly and sore – but they are sentient beings, capable of feeling pain, suffering and depression. It's important to ask ourselves, are they still happy? And what would they want?

The rest of this section describes euthanasia and my experience of it, but if you are not feeling this kind of chat right now, feel free to skip ahead.

The two most common ways of euthanising a dog are to have it done in the vet's practice or in your own home. If your dog has always been terrified of the vet's, I would insist on a home visit.

My last dog always enjoyed visiting the vet and they are just a two-minute car ride away, so we felt ok to take her there. I made sure they knew why she was coming and the reception staff ushered me into a side room straight away, so I didn't have to sit waiting in reception. I was seen at a quiet time of day and the vet came straight away. She was so compassionate, and I remember her telling me what a kind and caring thing I was doing for my dog – that she was tired and so beautiful (and she was – gosh, it's hard writing this). I remember how hearing these things made me feel better, as I was still thinking she could maybe go on another month. But she wasn't happy; she didn't even want to look at her tennis ball, which she used to live for – she loved having that ball in her mouth, puffing it up and down with her jaw, and playing with the other dogs . . .

We laid her out on the vet's floor on a bed and her head was on my lap. We talked, and I told her how much we all loved her. It was so fast – she just closed her eyes peacefully. I obviously then sobbed and sobbed, but the staff were lovely and left me alone with her for as long as I needed.

When it was time to go, they didn't ask me to stand in reception and settle up or linger; I was just told to call back whenever I was ready. It was as peaceful and humane as I could have hoped.

I knew that I wanted her ashes in a casket (like my other pets – in case we ever move house, they will all always be with us). But if you don't wish for your pet to be cremated, you can take them away with you and bury them yourself; just check with your local authority for restrictions and rules in your area.

Dealing With Grief

Your dog is a family member, so allow yourself time to grieve. Anyone who has loved and lost can easily understand the sadness of losing a beloved pet. Take some time off work and time for yourself. Some people feel better in a week or two, while for others it takes months or even years. Allow yourself time to process your grief; feeling lonely, unhappy and shocked are all normal.

If you find you are struggling, reach out and talk to people, sharing your experience. It's so true that talking helps and there are charities out there offering bereavement support, so don't be deterred from seeking further help (see Resources, p. 248).

Remember . . .

There are many beautiful ways of remembering pooch. You can plant a tree or a flower bed over their ashes – something beautiful that you can look at every day. And you can compile a memory box, full of photos, their collar and favourite things. If you love sewing, a quilt is a lovely, mindful project to spend time on and reminisce. Photo books are super easy to make online now, so why not pop all your favourite photos in a keepsake photo album? Or you could build a little memorial in your garden – I've seen some in the form of water features, which are so pretty, and I love the idea of the water flowing over the earth. If you want to keep them close to you every day, their ashes can be made into jewellery (rings, necklaces and earrings) or, if you are feeling brave and adventurous, even a tattoo!

Your dog is a gift that you can treasure for ten to fifteen years, give or take. So make the most of every day – just as your dog does, with their eternal optimism. Approach every day with gratitude and enthusiasm, and simply celebrate your fuzzy friend's life.

RESOURCES

Mindfulness and Meditation

helpguide.org/meditations/mind-ful-breathing-meditation.htm

mindworks.org

To Report Suspect Breeders

four-paws.org.uk/campaigns-topics/topics/companion-animals/report-illegal-puppy-traders

Understanding Body Language

dogtime.com/reference/dog-training/48563-alpha-dog-myth-dominance-training-mistreatment

rover.com/blog/dog-eye-contact/

aspca.org/pet-care/dog-care/common-dog-behavior-issues/aggression

Finding a Dog Trainer

imdt.uk.com/find-a-qualified-imdt-trainer

dogstrust.org.uk/dog-advice/training

Activities and Sports

thekennelclub.org.uk/dog-training/good-citizen-dog-training-scheme/taking-part-in-the-good-citizen-dog-training-scheme

releasethehounds.ca/canine-connection-8-fun-games-to-play-with-your-dog

thesprucepets.com/top-dog-sports-1118567

Finding a Groomer

groomersspotlight.com

dogdiscoveries.com/health/facts-about-dog-nails

Food and nutrition

allaboutdogfood.co.uk

battersea.org.uk/pet-advice/dog-care-advice/toxic-food-dogs

Eco-friendly Choices

onegreenplanet.org/
environment/eco-friendly-way-
to-dispose-dog-poop

Yoga with your dog

dogayoga.fit

petsyoga.com

Dog boarding

trustedhousesitters.com

rover.com

petsitters.org

narpsuk.co.uk

Travelling with your dog

www.gov.uk

www.travelnuity.com

www.europa.eu

www.eurotunnel.com

www.akc.org

Complementary therapies

The International Veterinary
Acupuncture Society: ivas.org

The Association of British
Veterinary Acupuncturists:
abva.co.uk/vet-area/
veterinary-acupuncture-training

i-a-v-c.com/en/academy/
animal-chiropractic

iaat.org.uk

robfellowsreiki.com

hiddenriverhealing.com/
the-healing-power-of-nature

rover.com/blog/actually-yoga-dog

petmd.com/dog/pet-lover/
4-simple-dog-massage-therapy-
techniques

Dog Health

thekennelclub.org.uk/health-
and-dog-care/health/getting-
started-with-health-testing-and-
screening

msd-animal-health-hub.co.uk/
KBPH/my-dog/vaccination/
schedules

Dealing With End of Life

journeyspet.com/pet-quality-
of-life-scale-calculator

bluecross.org.uk/
pet-bereavement-and-pet-loss

supportline.org.uk/problems/
pet-bereavement

Further Reading

*How Dogs Love Us: A
Neuroscientist and His Adopted
Dog Decode the Canine Brain*
by Gregory Berns

rvc.ac.uk/vetcompass/news/
rvc-study-reveals-extent-of-dog-
obesity-crisis-in-the-uk

eatingwell.com/article/7669367/
signs-your-dog-is-stressed-or-sad

theguardian.com/society/2019/
jan/15/dog-poop-bags-plastic-
alternatives

dogsnaturallymagazine.com/
reiki-for-dogs-5-techniques-you-
can-use-at-home/

books to help you live a good life

Join the conversation and tell
us how you live a #goodlife

🐦 @yellowkitebooks
📘 YellowKiteBooks
📌 Yellow Kite Books
📷 YellowKiteBooks